ESCAPING THE WINTER

Since she gave up full-time employment in 1987, Anne Mustoe has spent every winter abroad. She has personal experience of living for long periods in almost all of the countries she mentions in the book. She is a classical scholar and has run her own travel business, organizing specialist tours to classical sites in Greece, Italy, Turkey and Tunisia. She is internationally renowned for her best-selling cycling adventures: *A Bike Ride*, *Lone Traveller*, *Two Wheels in the Dust* and *Cleopatra's Needle* [all published by Virgin].

ESCAPING THE WINTER

All you need to know about spending the winter abroad

Anne Mustoe

This edition published in 2003 by

Virgin Books
Thames Wharf Studios
Rainville Road
London W6 9HA

ISBN 07535 0825 7

Design and typesetting by Phoenix Photosetting, Chatham, Kent

Printed and bound by Mackays of Chatham, Chatham, Kent

CONTENTS

INTRODUCTION: ROBINS OR SWALLOWS?

One Boxing Day morning we were taking a brisk family walk across the frosty common when we met a robin. His feathers were so fluffed up against the cold that he looked like a little red and brown pompon. A week later I was in Aswan, sitting in the evening on my verandah overlooking the Nile and watching the swallows dip and swoop in the fading light. It was neither hot nor cold. The climate was so perfect that I was completely unaware of temperature or humidity. I thought about it only when darkness fell and I realized that I was sitting there without a shawl or a cardigan and yet my body felt totally relaxed. There was not the slightest suggestion of a shiver. I was in Egypt on a brief package holiday and in a few days' time I should be back in England among the hypothermic robins. But on that balmy starlit night, I made up my mind that as soon as I was free to do it, I would follow the sensible swallows every autumn to their southern haunts.

Some people find the cold invigorating. They bundle themselves up in their boots and woollies and stride purposefully through the snow. They go on skiing holidays. This book is not for them. It is for those of you who, like myself, are sun-seeking swallows.

In 1987, I calculated that I could just afford to give up my regular job and, since then, I have spent every winter abroad in warmer climes. I have travelled east and west as well as south, living comfortably in hotels and invariably returning to find that I had more to my credit in the bank at the end of the winter than I had had at the beginning. 'Wintering abroad' is no longer the preserve of the wealthy. Anyone who knows how to organize it can enjoy a wonderful winter in the sun – and even save money in the process!

I realize that some of my readers will have considerably more travel experience than others. Some of you may think that I labour the obvious, while others may feel that I offer too little guidance in certain areas. I would say to the first group that, even after a lifetime of travel, I still find handbooks with check-lists extremely valuable. It's so easy to overlook something vital; and there are always a few tips to be picked up, even from the most elementary sources. As for the second group, I have tried to put down all the basics, with guidance on where to go for further information. Whether you have spent years overseas or are venturing abroad for the first time, there is no substitute for your own careful research. The harder you work in advance, the more you will enjoy your winter escape.

Few people need to be persuaded of the delights of a winter in the sun. When the icy winds tear the leaves from the trees, who has not dreamed of strolling at ease along the promenades of the Riviera, or bathing from a palm-fringed beach? These are the romantic clichés of winter travel. But there is a practical side to it as well. The health benefits are considerable, particularly for anyone who suffers from bronchial problems, rheumatism or stress-related illnesses. The simplicity of the life, with its freedom from domestic chores and routine social obligations, leaves considerable time for the pursuit of leisure interests, for the development of new skills, for writing that book you always thought you had it in you to write and, in general, for re-evaluating your life and planning for the future. A winter abroad gives space for thought. I know that some of my best ideas have come to me when I have been half a world away from the daily grind; and there is nothing like distance for putting problems into perspective.

On the financial side, you can hope to make a good profit if you let your own home, as it is possible to live in comfort abroad within the rent of a UK property. But even if you choose not to let your home, you may still make savings and end the winter slightly in pocket. You will be free of some of your biggest bills

– your winter heating and lighting, and probably the running of your car. Your wardrobe will be small, light and informal. And your food and drink in a bounteous climate, where the market-stalls groan with fresh produce and the local wines and spirits are comparatively cheap, will cost you less than your grocery bills at home.

In recent years, the pound sterling has been strong in relation to other currencies, so prices of hotels and meals abroad have been relatively cheap for the fortunate British. But even when sterling is weaker, there are still bargains to be found. It pays to keep an eye on the tourist rates listed in banks and newspapers, to see how currencies are faring. For instance, if the euro is strong in relation to the pound and prices on the Continent seem high, the US dollar or the Turkish lira may be going through a bad patch. This means that it would make financial sense to choose Florida or Antalya that winter rather than the Riviera. There will always be somewhere less expensive to go.

When all the practical benefits are added to the stimulus of getting to know new places, a new culture, new people and perhaps a new language, the project of spending a winter abroad becomes wonderfully enriching.

Some people may hesitate because they are not very keen on taking holidays. They are happily busy in their own routine at home and feel bored and uncomfortable when they are driven out of it for a fortnight a year. But a winter abroad is a completely different matter. There is ample time to establish an alternative routine, which can be equally enjoyable – to join the local golf club, get to know the best walks, make new friends, get involved in voluntary work and generally establish those small daily rituals which are so secure and comforting. In fact, routine is important. It gives a regular shape to the days when you are away from home for months on end. Without it, there can be a strange feeling of drift.

Others may hesitate because they are alone. But for single people, or couples whose family have left home and who now find life a little empty, the outdoor society of a warmer climate brings great opportunities for making new friends.

Everyone sits outside in the cafés, reading newspapers, writing postcards, playing dominoes, chatting, or simply watching the world go by. In marked contrast to the isolation of huddling alone by your own fireside, you will automatically be brought into daily contact with both locals and fellow travellers. They too will want to talk – compatriots because it's always reassuring to meet someone from home; the locals because they are usually more expansive, more openly inquisitive than we are, or because they want to practise their English. I have spent winters abroad on my own and been quite overwhelmed by the hospitality I have met. I have sometimes had to lock myself away in my hotel room to get a bit of privacy!

So who can escape the winter? Anyone who has the time. Anyone who is free of the necessity to attend a workplace every day of the year – pensioners, some self-employed people, the fortunate few with a private investment income, the unfortunate few with a redundancy payment, those with sufficient savings and those who are prepared to let their own homes and live on the proceeds. Wealth is not the deciding factor. Armed with the practical, step-by-step instructions in this handbook, anyone can do it who has the time and the willingness to try something new. So be bold! It's easier and cheaper than you think.

PART I   HOW TO DO IT

1 THE MAJOR DECISIONS

HOME OR HOTEL?
There are many handbooks on the market which deal with the purchase of property overseas and give advice on long-term or permanent residence. Many such properties are bought by pensioners or by people in mid-career, who wish to have a place in the sun for family holidays now and for use later as retirement homes. Owning your own place abroad has obvious attractions, but I wonder if those attractions are great enough to justify the trauma of selling your home and uprooting yourself from family, friends, neighbours, country – everything dear and familiar? It seems to me to be an enormous risk to take and it can stir up family resentment when parents go far away and set up house in a strange land. Although they may not admit it even to themselves, they often feel strangely abandoned and they will certainly worry about your health and safety.

The alternative is to keep your home and return to it every year in the spring. England can be lovely in the summer and, like the swallows, you will be able to enjoy the best of both worlds. Your family and friends will feel happier about an absence of only a few months and you will soon pick up the threads of your English life again. After a week at home, it will feel as if you have never been away – and the break will have done your relationships a world of good!

If you are not going to buy a permanent home, the alternatives are time-shares, renting a property, or living in hotels – and in the hotel category I include what are now called 'aparthotels', blocks of serviced, self-catering studios with restaurants, sports facilities and swimming pools attached.

Time-shares normally provide only a few weeks' occupation in each year and you might find it less expensive to buy a property outright than to buy the entitlement to live in a time-share for a number of months. The purchase always necessitates extreme caution and the services of a good lawyer, as operators in the time-share market have gained themselves a less than shining reputation. A time-share is a tie. If your agreement is not of the more sophisticated, flexible kind which offers occupancy in a choice of resorts, you will have to return to the same place year after year, or engage in the complications of sub-letting.

Renting a property for a single winter gives more flexibility and may be a good choice for a family or a group of friends. But the landlord and tenant legislation can be complicated and you would need to have a knowledge of local employment legislation if you were to take on a maid or a gardener. And without a maid and gardener, you would end up with as many chores abroad as you had at home, with the added difficulty of coping with them in a foreign language. Shopping in the supermarket may be easy enough. But how would you find and communicate with a local plumber if a pipe burst? There seem to me to be endless possible problems.

My first choice of accommodation by far is a comfortable hotel (or aparthotel) and this is the option on which the advice in this book is based. The advantages are numerous:

No domestic chores
No gardening
No maintenance costs or house insurance
Someone always at hand to deal with spent light bulbs, malfunctioning lavatory cisterns and broken springs
The safety of a protected building with night porters
Room service if you are feeling under the weather
Help at reception with local services, from doctors and dentists to taxis
Daily contact with other people
Use of public rooms and other facilities
Ease of receiving visits from family and friends without having to prepare their rooms and cook for them.

And the last, most important, advantage is the freedom to change hotel, or even resort, if it fails to come up to expectations. You are not tied to one place by a capital investment or a long-term tenancy agreement. You can even pack your bags and come home, if that is what you decide you really want to do!

Having spent some time in a resort, you may conclude that you like it enough to live there permanently. But it seems to me to be prudent to get to know its winter lifestyle really well before making a long-term commitment. One or two winters in the area will give you a sound knowledge of the local property market, either for purchase or for rental. Meanwhile, you will enjoy the comfort and flexibility of hotel life.

HOW LONG?

I find that the ideal period is four to six months, but so much depends on individual circumstances – family, state of health, outside commitments, even the needs of the garden!

To be really economical, three months is the minimum. The cost of the fares needs to be spread over at least that period; if you are hoping to let your home, it will not be worth the effort for less; and a three-month minimum stay produces attractive reductions in hotel tariffs. On the non-materialistic side, an absence of less than three months will be no escape from the English winter and will scarcely compensate for all the planning and research that went into the project. You will no sooner have settled into a comfortable routine, explored the possibilities of your chosen resort and started to make friends than it will be time to pack up and leave.

Beyond six months, complications may begin to arise over formal documentation, such as visas and driving licences, and over your tax status. Guidance on all these aspects of absence abroad will be given in the appropriate chapters. But technicalities apart, I have found from experience that my own affairs have ticked along quite nicely at home when I have been away for half the year or less. Longer absences have been more difficult to manage and the accumulation of domestic chores and paperwork on my return has left me almost wishing that I had never gone away!

Mid-November to Easter is the period which suits me best, as I can then enjoy two springs, the earlier one abroad and the English spring at home. But your own departure date will depend partly on whether or not you wish to be at home for Christmas; and your return may be influenced by how early the spring arrives in your own part of the country. The final decision is yours. But do bear in mind that it is always easier to come home earlier than planned than it is to extend your stay. If you return early, you will have an extremely useful blank period in your diary for getting things done, whereas a late return will entail endless correspondence and phone calls to postpone engagements. If in doubt, plan for a longer rather than a shorter absence.

INDEPENDENCE OR A PACKAGE?

Special mention must be made of the long-stay winter packages now offered by a number of travel firms. Most of them are designed for people of or near retirement age: Saga, Cosmos Golden Times, Thomas Cook Forever Young and Airtours Golden Years are examples. It is a flourishing, ever-growing market throughout Northern Europe and the United States. But comparative youth need not be a handicap. All the major tour operators will quote special rates for extended stays.

Some destinations – parts of the Costa del Sol and certain resorts in Malta, for example – are now so dominated by the major tour operators that there is little scope for the independent traveller. The tour companies offer the hotels a contract for the whole winter and are consequently able to insist on extremely favourable terms, which no individual could hope to match. Although most of the British contracts are with three- and four-star hotels, there are firms in Scandinavia and Germany which target the budget end of the market and snap up the rooms in smaller hotels and pensions. This makes it extremely difficult for the independent traveller even to find accommodation, let alone negotiate an off-season reduction. The only places which can be relied upon to have long-term vacancies are the luxury five-star hotels, as these are beyond the price-range of the package trade. So if Puerto de la Cruz on Tenerife or Albufeira in the Algarve is your chosen destination, you cannot do better than book a package with a reputable tour operator. A glance at two or three brochures will leave you in no doubt as to which countries and resorts are in thrall to the major operators and therefore inappropriate for independent travel.

Long-stay winter packages are usually available on a limited range of popular locations on the Algarve, the Canaries and the Costa del Sol, though Panorama Tours have now added Morocco, Tunisia and Cyprus to the list. Many cater for special interests, e.g. duplicate bridge, painting, botany or golf. All offer reliable service in a smart hotel or apartment block (an aparthotel), on half board or self-catering terms, with companionship and organized leisure activities. Flights and transfers to and from the hotel are always included, as are the services of resident English staff. Packages to the USA generally include car hire, and many special-interest packages offer discounted participation rates. Golf holidays, for example, can save considerable expense by including temporary membership of the local club and entitlement to a free round every day.

As most of the hotels and self-catering aparthotels used by the British tour operators have a high star-rating, the packages are not inexpensive, though they represent excellent value for money. They offer a safe and trouble-free way of wintering abroad. Careful comparison of their prices in the various resorts can result in a winter abroad which costs little more than staying at home and keeping the house warm. But the real economies are made by those who travel independently to less popular resorts.

Whether you buy a package or not will be influenced partly by the hotel situation in your chosen resort and partly by the size of your disposable income. But the real deciding factor will be yourself – the kind of person you are, your interests and your preferred lifestyle. Perhaps the following questions will help you decide:

Do you like everything to be organized for you, or do you positively enjoy making your own arrangements?

Do you like to live with a group of your fellow countrymen, or do you prefer to move among the local people and find your own friends?

Are you willing to work at the language before you go, so that you can at least scrape by on your own, or do you prefer to live in an environment geared to the British, where no foreign languages are needed?

Do you have a strong preference for English food, or do you like to experiment in the local restaurants? (Most package hotels have a buffet service with a choice of English and familiar Continental dishes, which obviates both menu and language difficulties – and saves the hotel money on waiters!)

How much travel experience have you had?

Are you so keen on, say, golf or bridge that you need to join a special-interest package?

Some travellers are put off by what they perceive as the enforced jollity of winter packages, with aerobics in the morning and sequence dancing at night. But these activities are all optional and those who enjoy quieter pleasures can always go off for a solitary walk, join a bridge club or make local friends. The art of the package holiday is to take advantage of the convenience and low basic cost, while retaining freedom of action. When the whole winter is such a bargain, an occasional weekend away from the group or a few meals out in good local restaurants are easily affordable diversions. But read the brochures carefully before you choose. Travel agents, like estate agents, have their own special vocabulary. For instance, resorts described as 'lively' are generally at the disco, lager and chips end of the market!

Going it alone takes considerably more forward planning, but rising to a new challenge brings tremendous satisfaction. The more work you put into an enterprise, the more rewarding it becomes. If you have not spent the winter abroad before, an organized package may well be the ideal halfway house. Then, if the lifestyle appeals to you, you might consider making an independent arrangement for the following year. Or if you are drawn to an exotic destination, but feel understandably apprehensive about going alone, try a fortnight's package holiday in advance. It will give you the feel of the place and the climate and enable you to decide whether or not you could cope there on your own.

Most of the information provided in this handbook will be of assistance to both the long-term package-taker and the independent traveller. Only the sections on choice of hotel and price-bargaining are written specifically for those who venture forth alone.

2 FORWARD PLANNING

DATES

Choosing the date for departure can be one of the trickiest aspects of the whole project, because it raises the thorny question of what to do about Christmas. If you decide to spend it abroad, family reaction can range from scarcely concealed delight that they will be free to celebrate Christmas as and where they like, without reference to you, to genuine dismay.

I started to go away for Christmas many years ago. At first, I went abroad alternate years, making it clear that I should be at home the following year. That was a useful beginning. The family were reasonably happy about it and came to enjoy running their own festivities. Now I get a warm invitation to attend, but no one is surprised or upset if I turn it down in favour of Christmas in the sun.

If you have never been absent at Christmas before, you might find this a tactful approach. Another palliative might be to invite them to join you for Christmas in your hotel, distance permitting. However you handle it, the situation may be a little tense, but it pays to persevere. It will be much easier next time. And you should persevere with a clear conscience. After years of duty well done, you are surely entitled to please yourselves once in a while!

Once you have decided on your ideal departure date and the length of time you can spare, *put firm lines through the relevant weeks in your diary* and make no further appointments for that period. It may seem an obvious piece of advice, but if you are not very strong in your resolution, your arm will be twisted and temptations put in your way. Your leisurely winter in the sun will gradually be whittled down to a few rushed weeks.

THE SCHEDULE

I always find it useful to draw up a schedule of the arrangements I have to make, using a three-month frame and aiming to complete preparations as far in advance as possible. It helps to avoid missed deadlines and last-minute rushes. When the schedule is complete, it can be kept for another year, with amendments in the light of experience. Anticipation is one of the pleasures of wintering abroad. In fact, I usually find that I enjoy my preparations almost as much as the trip itself.

The schedule will tell you when you need to begin work on each aspect of your preparations, with deadline dates for the completion of each task. Aspects to be covered are:

Research and choice of destination (see Chapter 3)
Travel arrangements
Financial preparations (see Chapter 4)
Personal insurance (see Chapter 4)
Passports, visas and official checks (see Chapter 5)
Arrangements for correspondence
Medical preparations (see Chapter 8)
Letting or securing the house (see Chapter 6)
The car (see Chapter 7)
Pets
Learning the Language
Enrolling on other courses
Making a luggage list (see Chapter 9)
Listing last-minute jobs and safety checks.

Most of these headings are broad enough to warrant their own chapters, so I shall deal here only with the miscellaneous items.

RESEARCH AND CHOICE OF DESTINATION

Deciding the dates is the first priority. If you have still not made up your mind at that stage about your destination, there is plenty of preparatory work you can be doing – in fact, everything can be arranged except travel, insurance, inoculations and packing. So there is no need to feel rushed into that crucial decision. It is better to spend longer on your research than to decide on a country in a hurry and regret it. The deadline for your decision will probably be the last date for booking an Apex or other reduced-fare flight, though it is obviously advisable from every point of view to end the uncertainty long before that.

Once you have decided on your country, do continue to read as much about it as you can. If you have a good understanding of its culture, history, politics and people, you will adapt with ease to the lifestyle and feel at home from the very first week.

TRAVEL ARRANGEMENTS

Air Most people these days fly to their destination and if your chosen resort lies in another continent or on an Atlantic island, such as Madeira or the Canaries, there will be no convenient alternative. Thorough research into Apex fares, which have to be paid for two weeks in advance, budget airlines and special charter offers will pay dividends. But check carefully the duration of the ticket and the penalties, if any, for changing the date of the outward or return booking.

High street travel agents, whose main business is the marketing of package holidays, may be of limited assistance. To find the best bargains, consult one of the specialist firms, such as Trailfinders, 215 Kensington High Street, London W8 6BD. Tels: 020 7937 1234 (European) 020 7937 5400 (Transatlantic) www.trailfinders.co.uk or any branch of Thomas Cook or American Express, two firms with wide experience in catering for the individual traveller. The Sunday papers and the internet are good sources of information about discounted fares, but do exercise caution here and choose a member of ABTA.

Rail The new high-speed European supertrains can make the journey an enjoyable part of the holiday. France's TGV can whisk you down from Paris or Lille to Nice within the day; while Valencia is only fifteen hours away via Toulouse, the Pyrenees and Barcelona. Sleepers and couchettes are available to add to the comfort.

The great advantage of rail travel is its flexibility. Journeys can be broken at any point, to visit interesting cities en route or simply to rest overnight in a peaceful place. And should you have to change your plans, the fare is refundable, less a 10 per cent cancellation fee. This compares favourably with the conditions of issue for bargain air fares, where the full fare is often forfeit.

But there are many disadvantages, the chief one being cost. Apex fares are valid for two months only, which means that travellers going abroad for longer periods have to buy two full-rate singles. This usually works out more expensive than discounted or budget air fares. And the various rail passes on offer are of limited use. The Inter-Rail passes for young people are valid for one or two months only, depending on type. Rail Europe Senior Cards, available at £12 to holders of British Senior Railcards, are valid for a year and offer discounts of 30 per cent, but there are restrictions on their use for journeys *within* European countries, as distinct from journeys which cross frontiers. If you are a railway buff and still want to persevere with this option, you can get more detailed information from: Rail Europe Ltd, 179 Piccadilly, London W1. Tel: 0870 584 8848. www.raileurope.co.uk

Coach   Coaches are the Cinderellas of the travel trade, but for those who prefer not to fly, they are a most convenient and economical alternative. Eurolines runs direct services from Victoria Coach Station to over five hundred destinations in Europe and Morocco, where they link up with the local bus network. Return tickets are valid for six months and the return half may be issued as an open ticket, allowing maximum flexibility in the choice of return date.

Travelling by coach is much cheaper than the train. The current standard return on the coach to Nice, for example, is £95 as against £85 *each way* for the two singles you would have to buy on the train. And there is an additional saving of 10 per cent on the coach fares for young people (13–25) and seniors (over 60), which brings the price down to £86 return, just half the train fare. Refunds of 50 to 80 per cent are available on cancelled tickets, depending on the notice given, and changes of date are allowed.

But the greatest merit of the coach is its simplicity. Once you have boarded your coach at Victoria, your journey to your destination is smooth and well organized. The coaches are comfortable, with on-board toilet facilities and reclining seats, and there are regular refreshment stops. If the coach uses one of the Channel ferries, your luggage stays on board. Any transfers take place in bus stations with the assistance of Eurolines staff. The down side is that overnight travel on a coach can be tiring, particularly for those with long legs.   But there are always hotels near bus stations, if you prefer to break your journey.

National Express and Caledonian Express act as agents for Eurolines (UK) Ltd, so that tickets for the international services can be booked at any bus station. Bookings can also be made online at eurolines.co.uk or by calling 08705 143219 any day between 8.00 a.m. and 10 p.m. All Eurolines services are Government approved.

For the impecunious traveller, cheaper coach services are available. These so-called 'magic buses' are advertised in *Time Out*, the *London Evening Standard* and other journals. Most of the services operate within the law, but a few 'cowboy' enterprises flout the local safety regulations. Careful enquiries about the number of drivers to a coach need to be made before booking.

Car   Travel by car will be dealt with in Chapter 7.

ARRANGEMENTS FOR CORRESPONDENCE

About a month before your departure, it is a good idea to send round a duplicated letter or card, informing friends and associates of your plans for the winter and giving the dates of your absence. (If you are leaving anywhere near to Christmas, you can save postage by sending out this note with your Christmas cards; if you are leaving earlier, it will exempt you from sending Christmas cards at all!) The circular should include the name, address and telephone number of a member of your family or a close friend, who has agreed to act as your contact. If that person is given your overseas address and phone number as soon as you are settled, (s)he can pass on the information to anyone who needs to get in touch with you. The sending of this circular will automatically reduce the amount of correspondence sent to your home and will serve as your apologies for any committee meetings.

Bills and cheques are dealt with under Financial Matters in Chapter 4. If these are taken care of, and personal and business correspondence forestalled by the circular letter, the envelopes which fall through your letter-box will contain little other than junk mail. But though these letters may not be important, they should at least be picked up. If an envelope gets wedged in the letter-box, or if a pile of envelopes is visible through a glass door, you are advertising the fact that you are away from home. There are two ways of dealing with the matter. One is to arrange for the Post Office to forward your residual mail to a relation or friend. Application forms for this service are available from any post office and the current charges are £6.30 for a month, £13.65 for three months and £21.00 for six months. These charges apply only to re-direction within the United Kingdom. You *can* have your letters sent on to you abroad, but the Post Office will make an extra charge. If you feel that you cannot live without your mail, it is probably simpler and quicker for your friend to send it out to you in occasional packets and pay the postage.

The other way of overcoming the difficulty is to arrange for your relation or friend to call regularly at your home. This will also add to your peace of mind, as you will know that someone you trust is visiting your home and keeping a general eye on it.

Whether or not you ask your friend to open your mail will obviously depend on your relationship and on how confidential you like to keep your affairs. But whatever the arrangement, do make it crystal clear, so as to avoid the kind of misunderstanding that can lead to resentment and ill-feeling. Your friend should know in advance whether you wish him to:

(a) open all the mail, deal with any bills and cheques and inform you of important items;
(b) open only the Visa and Access statement and any other envelopes which clearly contain bills, in order to deal with them in the agreed manner;
(c) open nothing.

If you have prepared your winter escape carefully, there should be little of consequence in the post and your friend's responsibilities should be light. But they will be worth at least a bottle of Scotch from the Duty Free!

PETS

Taking little Fido or Fluffy abroad is still quite a complicated business, despite the new Pet Travel Scheme. Your dog or cat will need to be fitted with a microchip, vaccinated against rabies, have a blood test, be treated against ticks and tapeworm and issued with special certificates. There are restrictions on the mode of travel and the routes which may be used; and the Scheme applies only to listed participating countries. Getting your pet back home again involves yet another set of regulations.

The good news is that the staff at D.E.F.R.A. (Department for Environment, Food and Rural Affairs) are extremely helpful. They will send you a comprehensive information pack – and even phone you back when you leave a message! They are to be found at: Area 201, 1A Page Street, London. SW1P 4PQ. PETS Helpline: 0870 241 1710. www.pets.helpline@defra.gsi.gov.uk

However much you love them, you may well decide not to take your pets on your winter escape. So you will need to make arrangements with a kennels, a cattery or a kind friend. For a long period you may be able to negotiate reduced kennel rates. Employing a house-sitter to take care of your pets in your own home is another possibility (see Chapter 6).

LEARNING THE LANGUAGE

If you are planning to spend the winter in a country where the native tongue is not English, it will add immeasurably to your enjoyment if you are able to communicate with the locals. It is not, of course, strictly necessary, because English is now the universal language and the staff in hotels, restaurants and airports will all understand you well enough to attend to your basic needs. But they will appreciate even a few simple greetings in their own language; and you will be much more independent if you can go so far as to ask the way or the price of goods in the shops. Even better, if you start well in advance, you may even reach the conversational level at which you can make local friends and understand the television news.

Classes   A number of courses are available to the adult learner. Signing on at the local college of further education can be useful, even if you can only attend for the first two-thirds of the autumn term before you go abroad. These courses are inexpensive and are offered at various levels, to suit everyone from the complete beginner to the advanced student who simply needs to brush up his conversational skills. Londoners are particularly well served, as they can study anything from French to Mandarin or Gujurati. The provision in other areas may be more limited, but most will offer courses in the more common European languages, plus a few of the more exotic.

Home Study   If you prefer to study at home in your own time, by far the best way to do it is to get yourself a language study pack, consisting of a book and tapes. There are dozens of these on the market and they are either on the shelves or available on order in most book shops. Or you can borrow them from your public library. For the more common languages, like French and Spanish, the BBC produces both beginners' and intermediate packs at £39.99 each. But there are well-tried, cheaper options, such as Hugo's *Spanish in Three Months* (or French, Portuguese, Turkish, or whatever) at £29.95 and a long list of languages in the *Teach Yourself* series, published by Hodder Headline at £22.95. All these courses cover grammar as well as practice in conversation. At a more basic level, the BBC's *Get by in . . .* range is excellent. I got by very successfully across China, in places like the Gobi Desert where no one spoke any English, on the very elementary grammar and listening practice in their *Get by in Mandarin* pack. It was £9.99 well spent.

Talking Phrase Books If you are the perfect example of English hopelessness at foreign languages, there is still some-thing you can do. At least buy a Berlitz or Collins phrase book for around £10. These days, the books come with a CD or tape, which you can play constantly in the car or doing the household chores. Without learning any grammar, you will pick up a few key phrases and be able to pronounce them correctly.

ENROLLING ON OTHER COURSES

English as a foreign language Most foreigners are keen to learn English and there is considerable scope for teaching it abroad. If you feel that you would like to help, it is necessary to be familiar with the direct method used in TEFL (Teaching English as a Foreign Language) or ESL (English as a Second Language). Readers of this handbook will not be looking for regular full-time employment abroad, so the investment of time and money involved in a lengthy full-time course would not be appropriate. Much more suitable are the short crash courses, lasting between one and four weeks, run by the com-mercial language schools. These usually take place during the summer holidays on university campuses at home and abroad and are very pleasant, if demanding, courses to attend. The longer courses lead to the Royal Society of Arts Certificate. Shorter ones are certified by the organizing language schools.

The EFL/Overseas sections of the *Times Educational Supplement* carries advertisements for these practical courses, as well as for a number which combine home study with weekend seminars. The larger TEFL companies, such as Linguarama, with its worldwide network of centres, offer teaching posts abroad to students who have successfully completed their courses. It might be useful to add a TEFL course to your schedule of preparations, but beware of contravening the local legislation by teaching without a permit (see Chapter 5).

Other courses A whole winter abroad will give you ample time to develop your own special interests. If you are a keen amateur photographer, if you have painting or craft skills, or if you fancy trying your hand at articles for newspapers, or even writing a book, why not enrol on the appropriate course at your local college before you go? You will hone your skills and you may even get some ideas on how to turn your hobby into an income-producing occupation.

LAST-MINUTE JOBS AND SAFETY CHECKS

We are all familiar with those panics which strike on the way to the airport. Did I switch off the cooker? Did I lock the back door? To ensure that those small, nagging doubts do not ruin your trip, begin well in advance to prepare two comprehensive check-lists. Keep them in a prominent place (on the fridge door?) and add to them, whenever a new item occurs to you. List One will contain all the jobs which need to be done in the last few days at home, while List Two will give the very final checks.

Everyone's lists will be different, but a few obvious examples for inclusion in List One will be: cancel the newspapers, milk and other regular deliveries; defrost the fridge; place jewellery and other valuables on safe deposit in the bank; take the cat to the cattery; deal with the indoor plants. List Two will be a reminder of all those vital last-minute jobs, such as switching off appliances, emptying the kettle and the rubbish, checking the windows and doors. Between them, the two lists will itemize all the boring little chores which you can so easily overlook – or, equally unnerving, think that you *may* have overlooked! When you know that you have gone round, lists in hand, and ticked off every single item on them, you will be able to sit back and enjoy the journey in utter peace of mind.

3 DESTINATIONS

CHOOSING YOUR COUNTRY

You may already have a favourite country towards which you will automatically gravitate, one which is familiar and much loved as a result of successful summer holidays there. Your first instinct may well be correct, but before making a final decision, sit down and list the advantages and disadvantages under a number of heads.

CLIMATE

The Mediterranean has an obvious pull for the peoples of Northern Europe. Compared with the English winter, the weather will on average be warmer, sunnier and drier almost anywhere along the Mediterranean coast, while some stretches, like the Riviera, the Costa del Sol and the southern coast of Turkey, which are sheltered from the north by significant mountain ranges, can be positively balmy much of the time. But whatever the holiday brochures say, the unvarnished truth is that you need to go down to about 30°N (i.e. to the latitude of Cairo) to be sure of warm weather all the time. And even there, it will rain, because winter is the rainy season. If reliable warm weather is your objective, you must go further afield – to the Canaries, to Florida, Thailand, Malaysia, southern Morocco or the southern hemisphere.

And a word of warning about islands. They are idyllic in the summer, because there is always a breeze from the sea to temper the burning heat. But in winter that same breeze can become an icy blast, which not only freezes the islanders to the marrow, but cuts them off from the outside world. I have been marooned for days on both Rhodes and Crete, when the wind has been too strong for either ferries or flights to operate.

COMMUNICATIONS WITH HOME

Consider the distance of your proposed winter home from the nearest airport. Could your family circumstances, complications in your financial affairs or your state of health necessitate an emergency trip to the UK? If so, a twelve-hour drive to an airport is out, as are small storm-girt islands with unreliable ferry services. Fortunately, telephone calls throughout the world are simple these days, with international direct dialling.

COMMUNICATIONS LOCALLY

Are there good local bus, train or ferry services? And are there places in the vicinity which are interesting to visit for a day or a weekend? Even paradise can become a little monotonous and a short expedition makes a welcome change. Islands, though agreeably intimate, are limited in scope, especially if they are far from the mainland.

FAMILY AND FRIENDS

Do you really want to 'get away from it all', or would you be pleased to have visits from family and friends? Your answer to this question will obviously influence your distance from home and the ease of travel. You should, incidentally, be able to do a deal with your hotel on the price of your visitors' accommodation.

COST

As a general rule, countries with a Western lifestyle charge Western prices and the more challenging the environment, the less the winter will cost. Account also needs to be taken of the fluctuations of sterling against other currencies. If the pound is low in relation to the dollar, a winter in California, or a cruise priced in dollars, might be better deferred to another year, in the hope of stronger sterling. When sterling is weak, it is better to look at the southern Mediterranean countries, which tend to share our currency problems, or to Eastern destinations, where the cost of living is generally so low that a fall in sterling makes little difference to their affordability.

HEALTH
Do you have a medical problem, which makes it inadvisable for you to live in a hot climate? Or a condition, like rheumatism, which would benefit from a particularly dry climate? Are there certain types of terrain which you should avoid? Very hilly resorts, such as Madeira, with steep cobbled streets and mountainous countryside could be difficult for anyone with cardiac or mobility problems.

LEISURE ACTIVITIES
Take a careful look at what is on offer. Do you play golf? Fish? Walk? Play bridge? Are you a keen churchgoer? As only the extremely hardy will wish to bathe in the Mediterranean between November and April, are there heated swimming pools? Are there cultural and archaeological sites within easy reach? Are there interesting gardens? Interesting flora and fauna? Whatever you enjoy doing, make sure that your chosen resort will have facilities for it. This is an important consideration in a long stay. A quiet resort may be perfect in the summer, when you are tired and can think of nothing more wonderful than lazing away a couple of weeks in a deck-chair by the pool. But even if you went far enough afield to escape cold snaps, you would have to be a really dedicated deck-chair lounger to be content with that sort of life for six months!

WORK
Do you have a skill to offer and would you be interested in finding paid work? If so, you need to research the possibilities and pay careful attention to the work-permit situation.

SOCIAL LIFE
The number of other British people, who are resident or are

wintering in a country, may be a very important consideration. Statistics are difficult to find, but I have done my best to give some information under this head in Part II. Some people need the company of fellow Britons in order to pass their days and evenings pleasantly. Others mingle very happily with Americans and Australians, but need to be in a country where English is the spoken language. Others are good linguists and are sufficiently self-contained to be happy in a strange environment, trying to make friends with the locals. A realistic assessment of your social needs is most important for the success of a winter abroad.

And a final small point – do you mind being stared at? If you go where the population has the same colour skin as your own, you will merge comfortably, until you open your mouth! In the East, a white face is an object of curiosity. Some people find this tiresome, while others are open to the possibilities for social contact which this curiosity provides. You need never feel alone in the East, as there will always be someone bursting to talk to you in English. But you may not enjoy being the odd one out.

SPIRIT OF ADVENTURE

If you are an experienced traveller, possibly one who has lived abroad, you will be open to any ideas. But if this is your first experiment with a long-term absence, you may prefer to take it gently and choose a familiar country nearer to home, or book a long-stay package holiday. Then, if your first winter is a success, you can graduate to more adventurous locations later.

GENERAL CRITERIA

In Part II some possible destinations are listed. The criteria for inclusion are:

   a warm winter climate
   good communications with home
   good internal communications for touring
   pleasant lifestyle

political stability
value for money.

It is by no means a comprehensive list. Other countries, such as Kenya, the Gambia and Mexico, might take your fancy and there is no reason why you should not spend a successful winter there. Just follow the guidelines set out in Part I and do your own research. The Foreign and Commonwealth Office are there to advise travellers on 020 7238 4503/4 or www.fco.gov.uk (click on Travel).

CHOOSING YOUR RESORT

A few recommendations are made in Part II, but there is no substitute for doing your own research and making your own choice. Once you have decided on your country, or made your final short-list, guide books, travel brochures and the appropriate government tourist office should be able to provide all the specific information you need. The experience of friends and the social introductions they may be able to provide are particularly useful. There are basically three options: town, country and seaside.

TOWNS

I am a 'townie', born and bred, and rarely feel happy for long away from the bustle and the intellectual excitement of a city. If you are that kind of person too, you will find what you are looking for in Mediterranean cities such as Valencia, Cannes or Antalya (all, incidentally, seaside resorts too); in Penang or Malacca out East; and in Miami or San Diego out West.

COUNTRY

Except in North Africa, where 'inland' means South into the Sahara, it is not advisable in the winter to stray far from the Mediterranean coast. Mountain ranges sweep down almost to the shoreline and an hour's drive uphill from, say, Cannes to

Brignoles or Valencia to the plains of La Mancha will take you from summer-dress weather to below freezing. To be sure of really warm, inland weather, you need to go to the tropics, the southern hemisphere or the southern states of America. But consider carefully the leisure activities on offer. Many country-lovers spend all their spare time cultivating their gardens. That hobby will not be available and you will need to be content with the study of wild flowers (Madeira and Malaysia's Cameron Highlands are good choices for this) or enjoy other occupations altogether. The old British hill stations and golfing meccas, such as Palm Springs, have good tourist facilities and a range of social activities; elsewhere, provision may be limited. 'The British build little houses up in the mountains and live there on their own,' said a puzzled Turk. 'They seem to like it!' If that is what you like too, head inland – but be careful of the climate.

SEASIDE

For the majority, this is the obvious choice. We British are a seafaring race and there is nothing we like better than a brisk walk along the beach or the promenade, breathing in the ozone. Fortunately, there is an infinite choice of resorts around the world. Whatever your taste – casinos and bright lights or sleepy fishing villages in untroubled coves – a little research should take you exactly where you want to be.

CHOOSING YOUR HOTEL

There has never been a better time to go it alone. Post September 11, the travel trade has taken a real battering, as people have been afraid to fly and nervous of venturing abroad. Hoteliers are so desperate for business, that prices have tumbled and are still tumbling fast. This makes it difficult to quote meaningful rates for recommended hotels. Government tourist offices suggest the direct approach, by phone, email or in person, as printed room-rates for hotels are just so much waste paper. There are so many great bargains out there that the independent traveller on a modest budget can afford a level of luxury that was previously out of reach. It's a buyer's market and it pays to bargain.

Your hotel will be your home for the next three to six months, so it needs to be a place where you will feel warm enough (or cool enough, depending on the climate), comfortable and relaxed. Take your time in reaching this most important decision. Inspect a number of hotels, choose with care and make sure that you negotiate a satisfactory rate.

Day One – On arrival at your chosen resort, you will probably feel tired and dishevelled after the journey. A bad experience with a hotel on that weary first night could colour your entire view of the place and your project. Whatever class of accommodation you have in mind for your winter stay, treat yourself to a really comfortable hotel for the first three or four nights. A clean, warm bed, spacious rooms and plenty of hot water will soon revive you and leave you ready to meet any challenge. To be a useful first base, the hotel should be centrally situated. It is a good idea to have a specific hotel in mind on arrival, so that you can dismiss importunate touts and summon a taxi with confidence. Part II recommends one such hotel in each location, which I have called the *Starter Hotel*. It is a reliable hotel in the middle of the price-range. Those who want something more luxurious can check into the nearest five-star hotel without difficulty. Those who wish to pay less in the longer term may need to spend a number of days searching for the right place. Meanwhile, the Starter Hotel will provide a comfortable, reasonably priced base. It makes life simpler to accept the official tariff without too much quibbling for the first few nights. If you like the Starter Hotel enough to make it your winter home, you can bargain later, when you have a sound knowledge of the competition.

Day Two – You may already have a map of the town and a list of hotels. If not, visit the local tourist office to obtain them. Then just wander around, adjusting to the climate and the time-change and getting your bearings. Watch the world go by over teas or coffees; in the evening, wander past the restaurants to see where the locals are eating; generally, get the feel of the place. By the end of this relaxing day, you will already have some ideas to follow up.

Day Three – Serious work begins. The recommendations in guide books are a good start, for although the prices will almost certainly be out of date, your book will give you some idea of comparative costs and value for money. Hotels come at all prices and the category you choose is up to you and your budget. But whether you are looking for five-star luxury or a basic pension, ask to see a room and examine it closely.

CHECK-LIST

(a) The hot water. Twenty-four hours a day? If not, when?

(b) Is there a bath or only a shower? If a shower, would the lack of a bath bother you long-term?

(c) Is there somewhere in the bathroom to drip-dry small articles of clothing?

(d) Does the lavatory flush properly?

(e) Is there central heating? What hours does it run? If there is no radiator, will the hotel provide some sort of room heater and include the cost of fuel in the normal hotel bill? Winter evenings are long and some form of heating is usually necessary.

(f) Are there sockets for your kettle, hairdryer or shaver?

(g) Is there a telephone in the room? This is useful for receiving calls from home or ringing home in an emergency. (For more on telephone options, see Chapter 10.)

(h) Furniture. Is the bed(s) comfortable? Is there at least one easy chair? Is there a table or dressing-table and chair suitable for writing? Is the lighting satisfactory?

Distinguish between essentials and trifles. For instance, if the handsome marble or woodblock floor is naked of bedside rugs, you can always buy cheap ones in the market and bequeath them to the hotel when you leave; but you cannot buy new beds.

(i) What is the general impression? Is the room light and spacious, or would it depress you on a grey day?

(j) What is the view from the window? Sea-views usually cost more; views of the back alley are cheaper, but may be dreary.

(k) Is there a pleasant area in the hotel, other than your bedroom, where you can sit and read or have a chat? Are there any leisure facilities?

(l) Most hotels these days have a television in every room. But is the one in your room capable of receiving BBC World and CNN? If not, is this facility available in a television lounge? Or is it possible to hire?

If you like the hotel, but not the room, ask to see others.

CLASS OF ACCOMMODATION

When deciding on the class of accommodation, there are a number of factors to consider, apart from the obvious one of price.

(a) Four- and five-star hotels are usually on the outskirts of towns or resorts. They are self-contained worlds, catering mostly for package and business travellers and serving international food. If you like to sample the local fare, you may need to take taxis into the town and back. Living in a lower star-rated hotel nearer to the town centre will give you a wider choice of restaurants, cafés and bars, as well as shops and cinemas, all within walking distance.

(b) Most five-star hotels have wonderful sports facilities – a heated swimming pool, a gymnasium, tennis courts, saunas and jacuzzis – but it is not always necessary to stay there to enjoy them. A modest entrance fee or a club subscription may give you access. The same applies to the evening whist drives, bingo or bridge, which many hotels put on for tourist groups. And their bookshops, coffee shops, restaurants, bars and shopping arcades are, of course, always open to non-residents.

(c) When considering an expensive hotel, ask yourself whether you really need all those extras you are paying for. Do you really want a television in your room, if the programmes are all in Turkish or Hindi? Do you really need their same-day laundry service? Their secretarial services? Their faxing facilities? Their little soaps, shampoos and shower-caps? And a mini-bar is superfluous, as you will soon set up your own private bar and be able to drink exactly what and when you like at a fraction of hotel prices. A hotel with one fewer star might suit your requirements just as well.

(d) Hotels with the best views over the sea or the mountains are usually the most expensive. But in winter the days are short and the weather may not be ideal for sitting out on your balcony. Perhaps you would be just as happy living a block away from the sea and saving £1 or £2 a night?

(e) The atmosphere of the hotel is important. Would you be happier, over a longer period, with personal family service, which gives friendly contact and a sense of belonging (but which *can* become tiresome and intrusive); or would you prefer a larger, less personal hotel, which gives a greater feeling of independence (but which *can* seem a bit lonely and cold)? The golden mean is probably the best, if you are lucky enough to find it – the hotel where you get a friendly greeting from reception, where you can stop for a chat with the proprietor or your fellow guests when you feel like it, but where no one is over-interested in your affairs.

(f) For those who really want to economize, a very simple hotel or pension is the answer, as it is always possible to sit and read in the warmth of the local cafés, spend happy days in the five-star hotels, enjoying their facilities – and in some countries even compensate for the lack of hot water by visiting the Turkish baths.

PRICE

You will normally be given the tariff for one night. If you like the hotel, explain that you are looking for a room for a number of months and ask for a reduction. Haggle! Say, politely, that you were hoping to find somewhere cheaper and offer no more than half the regular tariff. They may make a counter-offer, to which you will respond, until the point is reached where their price and yours are reasonably close. A useful bargaining-counter at this stage is breakfast. Agree to their price on condition that they include it. This can be the perfect compromise, as it obviously costs the hotel less to provide it than it would cost you to pay for it separately. If the hotel serves main meals, lunch or dinner could also become part of the deal. You will be a prize catch in the low season, so you can afford to be firm. If you are an older person or a teacher, two categories of people who are not always held in the highest regard at home, you may find that you are treated with great respect in many countries abroad. Your presence in the hotel will be a source of pride and may result in even better bargains!

The percentage reduction you may expect will, of course, vary with the season and the type of hotel. If it is *high season*, you may be lucky even to find a room, and 5 to 10 per cent off for a long stay would be the most you could expect to negotiate. *Out of season*, you should get a 35 per cent reduction – and you might well be able to negotiate 50, 60 or even 70 per cent off.

International chain hotels with salaried employees rarely offer more than a 15 per cent reduction, even in the lowest part of the low season; whether you take the room or not has no direct effect on the manager. Family-run hotels, on the other hand, even if they happen to be large multi-stars, will be much more accommodating. After all, it is *their* money and they will take the view that 'half a loaf is better than no bread'. The top end of the local market is often the best buy.

Much will depend on the circumstances of your particular case – the time of year, the type of hotel, the success of the season and even whether or not the proprietor likes the look of you! And remember that other people's losses are your gains. I have just come back from a journey through Turkey and the Middle East, and stayed in hotels where I was the only foreign tourist. For the traveller with an eye to a bargain, there is no better time than the present to spend a winter abroad. There are splendid opportunities out there for the brave!

DECISION-MAKING

By the time you have visited a number of hotels, you will have a good idea of the price-range and the facilities on offer. Some hotels will be able to quote their special rates immediately; others may have to consult an absent manager, in which case you will have to call later for the decision on reductions. But even if you obtain all the quotations on the first day, choose at your leisure. Tell the managers that you are looking at a number of possibilities and will come back later. That response may induce them to bring their offers down even further.

If you are lucky, you will have walked into a hotel and said 'This is the one!' But before you commit yourself, it pays to sit over a long coffee or lunch and make a careful comparison of value and comfort for money in all the hotels inspected. Then sleep on it. Your budget needs special care. An extra £1 a day may not sound a great deal, but taken over six months, it adds up to a substantial sum. And beware of small discomforts and shortcomings; they may seem trivial at first, but they can assume exaggerated importance over a period of time. It is important not to be rushed into accepting a room with which you are not entirely happy. Have the patience to begin the search again the next day and be prepared to invest a great deal of time and effort in the choice of what is, after all, your winter home.

ONE ROOM OR TWO?

Two people spending months on end in one hotel room need to get on extremely well! If the hotel you fancy is short of comfortable public areas, it might be worth your while to consider buying some privacy by taking two adjacent rooms. The hotel would almost certainly remove one of the beds from the second room and provide an extra chair or two, making the equivalent of a sitting room and bedroom with two bathrooms. You should expect a further substantial reduction on that option and it must be arranged as part of the initial deal. Two rooms in a small hotel might not work out much more expensive than one spacious one in a multi-star. Those preferring a self-catering aparthotel might consider a small two-roomed apartment rather than a large studio.

THE SINGLE TRAVELLER

Single travellers are penalized throughout the world. Single rooms, or doubles used as singles, rarely cost less than two-thirds of a double; and in countries which charge by the room, one person pays as much as a whole family. If you are going to spend a few months in a half-empty hotel, be tough! Start off by negotiating the reduction on a double, as if you were doing it on behalf of a couple, then ask them to halve that figure for a single. You may not succeed in your request, but you may bring the price down below the standard two-thirds of the double tariff.

THE PACKAGE TRAVELLER

Your hotel will be selected in advance from a brochure and your room will be allocated by the staff at the reception desk. It will probably be perfectly satisfactory, but if it falls below the standard you have been led to expect, do not hesitate to complain. Ask Reception to show you other rooms. And if you get no satisfaction from the hotel, go to the company representative, who may even move you to a more obliging hotel. You are a valuable long-term customer and your hotel room will be your home for the winter, so do not accept it unless you feel happy there.

4 FINANCIAL MATTERS

MONEY ABROAD

International finance is now so sophisticated that no one need worry about having sufficient funds when abroad. In most countries, obtaining money is as simple when you are away as it is at home. All you need is the credit balance in your bank account to start with! It is wise to have a number of sources of cash and credit available to you. The more, the better.

CASH

The spread of ATMs has revolutionized cash abroad. All you need is a piece of plastic, and you can get euros from a hole in the wall in any Greek or Spanish town, and Turkish liras in any seaside resort. It's one of the greatest marvels of modern technology. Cash machines abroad display the type of cards they will accept, just as they do at home – Visa, Mastercard and cards on the Cirrus, Maestro or Plus network – and they usually provide instructions in a choice of languages. Type in your regular PIN number and they will produce the cash, charging the amount directly to your account at home.

There will, of course, be occasions when the machines don't work or you need a small amount of cash to tide you over, so it's as well to take about £500 per person for a long winter escape in a mixture of pounds sterling and dollars. These should be carried in a variety of denominations, with plenty of smaller notes.

The dollar is now *the* international currency, welcome throughout the world. For the traveller, it has the added advantage of really low denomination notes. A £5 sterling note is the smallest amount that can be exchanged and that is sometimes too much. A $1 bill is the perfect amount for a small tip, or for that last cup of coffee in the airport before leaving for home.

A small amount of the local currency is always useful, to pay for a bus or taxi on arrival. You will find banks at your destination, at the airports or other points of entry, but a good tip is to check out the exchange rates in department stores before you leave. The larger branches of Marks & Spencer and John Lewis often change money at more favourable rates than banks and currency kiosks, either at home or abroad.

TRAVELLER'S CHEQUES

These are a safer form of ready money, replaceable if lost or stolen, provided the list of numbers has been kept separately. Thomas Cook and American Express are the best known and it is worth making an effort to get those cheques, if you are travelling to a less developed country. American Express dollar traveller's cheques can be used as cash in American hotels, restaurants and retail outlets. Sterling traveller's cheques are acceptable throughout the world, though countries outside Europe are more used to dealing in dollars. For all countries except the USA, where dollar cheques are obviously much more convenient, it is a matter of personal preference whether you take the bulk of your money in sterling or dollars. There are, however, two points to bear in mind:

1. When you buy dollar traveller's cheques, you are converting sterling into dollars. Then, when you use your cheques to buy Thai bahts, for example, you are converting dollars into bahts. You are therefore exchanging your currency twice, which is more expensive than making one exchange, from sterling directly into bahts.

2. It is advantageous to keep an eye on the international money market. If the pound is going through a bad patch and is on the slide against the dollar, the advantage of holding traveller's cheques in dollars, the stronger currency, may outweigh the disadvantage of the double exchange described above.

Whichever you decide on, it is important to get a mix of denominations – 50s or 100s for normal use, with a few cheques of smaller denominations to meet special requirements. The larger cheques are cheaper to buy.

How much money you take with you in this form will depend partly on the availability of ATMs and partly on your own preferences. If you normally settle most of your bills by credit, debit or charge card, and you are staying in a country where these are readily accepted, you may find that you can dispense with traveller's cheques altogether. But research the situation in your chosen destination carefully. If in doubt, take an emergency supply.

CHEQUES

Some retailers with international contacts are happy to accept payment by sterling cheque for large items, such as carpets. They will take a cheque drawn on your UK account. Have your calculator handy to double-check their conversion and, if it is a country with a relatively weak currency, ask for a small discount for your sterling.

CREDIT, DEBIT AND CHARGE CARDS

These are accepted in cities worldwide and are the easiest way of all to settle your bills. Credit and debit cards can also be used to obtain cash advances from banks and ATMs.

Credit cards   The chief issuers are Visa and MasterCard. Some countries have a preference for Visa, while others prefer MasterCard, so it is a good idea to carry both. You will need to make arrangements at home for your monthly statements to be cleared (see Money at Home below), if you are not to run up enormous interest charges.

Debit cards   As purchases and cash withdrawals are debited directly to your bank account, there is not the same problem with accumulating statement debts as there is with credit cards. The rates of exchange and handling charges are the same as those on credit cards from the same issuer.

Charge cards   The main issuers are American Express and Diners Club. These cards can be used in many hotels and retail outlets abroad, though they are less popular than Visa and MasterCard, as the commission they charge the retailer is substantially higher. If you hold an American Express card and have your cheque book with you, American Express offices will make a cash advance on a cheque drawn on your British bank account.

BANK DRAFTS AND INTERNATIONAL TRANSFERS

Computers and faxes make it very simple to transmit large sums of money from one country to another. If you had a real emergency, such as a large hospital bill, which it was impossible to pay by credit card or cheque, you would need to go to a local bank and arrange for the money to be wired out to you. Most of the UK banks and major building societies have their contacts overseas and it would be useful to find out in advance from your own bank the name(s) of the bank(s) in your chosen country with which they usually deal. That might speed up the transmission process in an emergency. Despite its technical simplicity, this bank-to-bank transmission of money is for some reason expensive to the customer. It is also inexplicably slow, sometimes taking several days, and it is not wholly dependable; faxes and drafts have been known to get lost in the pipeline. It is clearly a last resort, to be used only when all other methods fail.

HANDLING CHARGES AND COMMISSION

The discussion of the various types of facility has been limited to their relative convenience. Their relative cost is too complex an issue to be examined in depth in a handbook of this size. The rate of exchange on traveller's cheques, for instance, is generally more favourable than the rate on cash. But against this must be set the fact that traveller's cheques are prepaid, so that the bank has interest-free use of your money until the cheques are cashed. The main attraction of credit, debit and charge cards, is that no money is paid by the user until expenses are actually incurred.

The rate of exchange is calculated on the day the debit is transferred to the UK, at the rate prevailing on the London market for large sums. The issuing banks then add a charge, which varies from bank to bank, but the total cost of the exchange is still normally more advantageous to the traveller than that applying to traveller's cheques. If you have paid in advance for a half-board package, your out-of-pocket expenses will be relatively low and the difference in handling charges and commissions will be less important. But independent travellers, who will be paying for everything as they go along, could save money by looking carefully into the real cost of the various sources of foreign money available to them.

A FEW GENERAL POINTS

Always 'shop around' when changing money. There are many legitimate money-changers apart from banks (e.g. travel agents, jewellers, exchange shops) and they will all have their current rates on display. It is often more profitable, and it certainly saves queuing time, to change money in these shops rather than at a bank. Changing money in hotels is very convenient, but the rate of exchange is usually poor. Watch the commission charged as well as the exchange rate offered, as some dealers may offer a better rate, but recoup the difference by exacting a higher percentage commission, or setting an unreasonable minimum charge.

Avoid the black market, if it exists. The dealers may offer you a better rate of exchange, but the transaction will be illegal and you will have no means of redress if you are cheated. It is not worth the risk of arrest, or being swindled, for the sake of a few pence. Black markets exist only in countries where the banks set an unrealistically low rate of exchange and/or the currency is not fully convertible. Hard currency is consequently much sought after. You will have to be politely firm when you are approached by the cloak-and-dagger dealers. The problem does not, of course, arise in the advanced Western economies.

Where the local currency is stable, it pays to change money in large amounts, as commission is saved. When the local currency is weak and inflation rampant, it is better to change money in relatively small amounts – £50 at a time for those on packages and a week to ten days' expenditure at a time for those paying their own bills. You will then get a better rate of exchange for your sterling or dollars every time you buy a new supply of the local currency.

Keep a number of receipts for currency exchanged, if you are spending the winter outside the EC. Those needing to change some of their local currency back into sterling or dollars may have to produce evidence that they bought it with sterling or dollars in the first place.

Always keep your cheque cards separate from your cheque books and your traveller's cheques separate from the list of their numbers. Distribute your cash between a number of different wallets, pockets and locked receptacles; a money-belt is a very good investment. Particularly in poorer countries, avoid any display of wealth. Keep only the money you need for the day handy in your pocket or handbag. Producing a huge wad of notes to pay for a cup of coffee is asking for unpopularity or cadging, if not for serious trouble.

The prestigious gold card is not a good idea when travelling, as it only serves to advertise your affluence and make you a target for extortion. Gold cards are particularly popular with thieves and there are highly organized card-thieving rings in the East. The standard credit card is perfectly adequate for most travellers' needs.

It is one of the pleasures of a short holiday to spend freely, but a budget is essential for a whole winter abroad; otherwise expenditure will run out of control. Try to decide in advance roughly how much you can afford to spend each week, then either draw out that predetermined amount regularly, or change the appropriate number of traveller's cheques.

Beware of credit, debit and charge cards. When you are not at home to check the statements and see the way the expenditure is mounting up, month on month, it is only too easy for the facility to run wild and ruin your finances. Your 'flexible friends' are certainly flexible, but they may turn out to be less than friendly! You may decide that they are best kept for luxuries, gifts, excursions and emergencies.

MONEY AT HOME
Your financial affairs need to be left in good order to prevent problems arising during your absence. Examine them carefully three months before departure, so that you may have time to rationalize them, if necessary.

PAYING THE BILLS
You will need to leave sufficient money in your accounts at home to cover:

  debit card debts
  charge card debts
  credit card debts
  regular bills, such as utilities, mortgage payments
  contingencies.

By far the easiest way to deal with all these outgoings is by direct debit, standing order or monthly payment schemes. If you do not already have these arrangements in place, now is the time to make them. Those who feel happier in the ordinary way scrutinizing their bills before they pay them, can easily cancel the direct debit or other arrangements on their return. Gas and electricity bills will in any case need to be adjusted, as the estimated consumption will exceed the actual.

Contingencies may require an extra few hundred pounds in your current account, over and above your budgeted outgoings for the winter. The larger reserve funds, for which you might need to wire in an emergency, are better left in a deposit or savings account, where they will earn interest. There must, however, be ready access, not a long period of notice for withdrawals.

Careful forward planning will ensure that the number of bills left for your relation or friend to deal with will be minimal. They can be paid in one of four ways:

1. As there will normally be sufficient time between the arrival of the invoice and the last date for payment, your friend can ring you and ask you to post a cheque to him in the correct amount.
2. You can leave behind a small number of signed, crossed cheques, and your friend can fill in the payee and the appropriate sums.
3. You can pay your friend a lump sum in advance, from which the money may be drawn as required.
4. You can make arrangements with your bank or building society, empowering your friend to sign, on your behalf, cheques drawn on your own bank account.

It goes without saying that your friend must keep all statements and a formal account of any money which he receives and spends on your behalf.

RECEIVING INCOME

The more income that can be paid directly into your bank or building society account the better. There is no point in leaving cheques unbanked, when the money could be earning interest.

Company pensions are usually paid straight into the bank and it is possible to make the same arrangement for State pensions and some other benefits (see below). Income from Government bonds and building societies can also be credited directly to your account. If you have shares in a number of companies, the flurry of dividend cheques will place an unnecessary burden on the friend who deals with your post, so do arrange with the registrars of those companies for the dividends to be sent direct to your bank. Your friend will need your paying-in book for the odd cheque.

INFORMATION

To make life simpler for your friend, you should hand him a list of your bank accounts, savings accounts, insurance policies and company shares, with their reference numbers, also your National Insurance number. You should hand over to him any correspondence relating to unfinished business, with clear instructions as to any action you wish him to take. If a list of your account and policy numbers is not lodged with your will, this would be a good opportunity to rectify the omission, as photocopies are easily made.

PENSIONS AND BENEFITS

STATE PENSIONS AND BENEFITS

State retirement pensions, invalidity benefits and widow's benefits can be paid direct into your UK bank or building society account. You can choose to be paid every four weeks or every thirteen weeks. If you are going to be abroad for a few months during the winter, this is obviously the simplest course and it is in line with the general policy of arranging for as many payments and withdrawals as possible to be made directly into or out of your account. It is also the most convenient method, as it ensures a regular supply of money into your bank account to meet your standing orders, direct debits and miscellaneous bills. Form BR436C, obtainable from your local DSS office, gives the details of the arrangement, together with an application form.

It is in fact possible to arrange for retirement pensions and widow's benefits to be paid to you in some countries abroad, either four-weekly or thirteen-weekly, at the same rate that would be paid to you in the UK, but it hardly seems worthwhile for a few months' stay. Leaflets SA29 *Your Social Security*

Insurance, Benefits and Health Care Rights in the European Community and GL29 *Going Abroad and Social Security Benefits* give all the necessary information. These leaflets and any further advice you may need are obtainable from your local DSS office. Or you can order them from the department's website: www.dwp.gov.uk/publications.

PRIVATE OCCUPATIONAL PENSIONS

These are no doubt already paid direct into your bank or building society. If they are not, the necessary arrangements should be made with the company.

JOBSEEKER'S ALLOWANCE

If you are currently unemployed, and already in receipt of a contribution-based Jobseeker's Allowance, you may continue to receive it in member states of the European Community, provided you can demonstrate that you are seriously seeking employment. It is not an expenses-paid winter holiday! Your allowance must be contribution-based, not income-based. As it takes some time to set up this arrangement, you should start making enquiries early. Leaflet JSAL6 from your local Job Centre gives outline details, which you can discuss with the staff there.

PAYMENT OF NATIONAL INSURANCE CONTRIBUTIONS

If you are a self-employed person, paying the UK self-employed earner's contributions, and you go abroad for less than twelve months, you will continue to belong to the UK National Insurance scheme, even though you may be earning money abroad. You should therefore make arrangements for your regular contributions to be made during your absence. See Leaflet SA 29. If you are undertaking employment abroad, either for a UK or a foreign employer and you at present pay National Insurance contributions, you must contact the DSS, Pensions and Overseas Benefits Directorate, Newcastle upon Tyne, NE98 1BA. (Tel. 0191 218 7777), to clarify your position. The regulations vary from country to country and are outside the scope of this handbook.

PAYMENT OF PRIVATE INSURANCE PREMIUMS
These payments must of course be kept up during your absence, preferably by standing order or direct debit.

TAXATION
Generally speaking, if you spend up to six months abroad in the winter and come home for the rest of the year, your tax status is unaffected. You remain liable to UK tax on all your income, so you will have to complete your tax returns and pay your tax bills in the normal way. You will still be regarded as resident in the United Kingdom for tax purposes.

There are certain tax advantages to be gained from establishing non-residence, particularly in relation to capital gains tax and inheritance tax. Leaflet IR20, *Residents and non-residents – liability to tax in the UK*, deals with this matter. It can be obtained from your local tax office, from the Inland Revenue telephone order line 08459 000404, or by logging on to www.inlandrevenue.gov.uk.leaflets. It is most unlikely that those spending a winter abroad will even begin to fall into the non-resident category. But if you are self-employed, spending your winters out of the UK and being technically domiciled overseas, could become part of a useful financial strategy. You would need to seek professional advice, as the legislation is complex. It is not within the scope of this handbook to offer guidance on such arcane matters.

INCOME ARISING WITHIN THE UNITED KINGDOM
Both earned and unearned income should be declared, as usual, on your annual tax return.

EARNED INCOME ARISING ABROAD
Regular taxed income   If the work undertaken is of a regular

nature, such as a part-time post in a school or travel office, you may receive a salary which has been taxed at source. In that case, you should declare your gross earnings on your UK tax return and also the amount of tax deducted by your employer. Under the double taxation agreements, the income tax you have paid abroad will be set against your liability to UK tax. Official receipts and all other relevant documents should be kept, in case they are required by your local tax inspector. The local tax office can provide an up-to-date list of the countries with which the United Kingdom has entered into a double taxation agreement.

Occasional untaxed income   If you receive a fee for a casual work assignment, a newspaper article, for example, or a set of photographs which are published locally, this money will probably be paid to you gross, without deduction of local income tax. There is a widely held belief that such earnings are exempt from UK income tax, provided they are not sent or brought into the United Kingdom. This is not in fact the case. Even if you spend the money abroad, leave it on deposit in an overseas bank account for future use, or invest it in an offshore fund, you are still required to declare the earnings on your annual income tax return and pay UK tax on it.

A FINAL REMINDER

If one of your annual income tax payments is due on 1st January, remember to send a post-dated cheque in the correct amount to the Inland Revenue before you leave home.

HOLIDAY INSURANCE

Health Insurance is considered in detail in Chapter 8 on Medical Matters, House Insurance in Chapter 6 on Letting and Insuring your Home and Car Insurance in Chapter 7. This section deals with the rest of the personal cover provided through standard travel insurance schemes.

When we go on holiday, most of us take the easy course and arrange our travel insurance through our travel agents at the same time as we pay the deposit on our tickets. If you are booking your long winter escape as a package holiday organized by one of the specialist firms, it is probably simplest to stick to this practice and sign up for the firm's own comprehensive insurance cover. The company will have tailored the cover to suit their customers' requirements in the light of experience, and the local representatives will be familiar with the details of the policy and will consequently be able to provide prompt assistance in an emergency. Just check the small print to ensure that you are not excluded from cover on grounds of age, state of health, pregnancy, or because you wish to pursue a high-risk sporting activity. There may be additions to the premium in these cases.

If you are travelling independently, you would do well to examine, item by item, the insurance cover offered by the agency through whom you book your travel tickets. You may find that it does not meet your requirements in a number of ways.

Some types of insurance cover are essential:

1. *Medical Insurance* (see Chapter 8).
2. *Personal Accident*, usually £15,000 to £25,000 to cover your own death or disability.
3. *Personal Liability*, usually £1 to 2 million. This covers your legal liability for accidental injury to third parties or damage to their belongings. (It does not cover third party motor insurance, which must be paid for separately.) Some countries, notably the United States, have become extremely litigious; people may sue you for anything from accidental homicide to spilling a bowl of soup down a new suit. So be well covered. Also ensure that you have a fund of money available on call at home, as you may have to settle immediately and claim from the insurance firm later.
4. *Legal expenses* It is well to be covered for £20,000 to £30,000, in case you yourself incur legal costs in pursuing claims against a third party, relating to damage to property, injury, illness or death.

The remaining elements in the cover offered to you may be too high, or may not be required at all.

1. *Cancellation cover* If you are travelling by car or train, this may not be necessary. The cost of train and car-ferry tickets is refundable and all you stand to lose is the price of any seat reservations and a small administration charge, usually about 10 per cent. This may be less than the cost of the cover.

2. *Journey and baggage delay* As you will have all the time in the world, you will probably not need this cover at all.

3. *Baggage and personal effects* The total cover offered may be far too high. If you are wise, you will leave most of your jewellery behind in the bank vaults; while the odd ring or brooch that you do take may in any case be insured under your household policy through an 'all risks' provision. The same may well apply to your camera and binoculars. You may also have cover already for the loss or theft of your credit cards. Check up on your requirements before you go and on the state of your existing cover under other policies. You may not need special baggage insurance at all. And if you do, you may need more than the usual maximum cover of £200 an item.

4. *Money* The cover offered may be less than you need for a long stay. Only cash needs to be insured, as traveller's cheques are replaceable without penalty.

PREMIUMS FOR LONG-TERM COVER

It is necessary to examine the method used by the insurers to calculate cover for a long stay. Some firms offer a policy for one month, then demand an additional premium for every week thereafter. Others increase the premium up to two months, then charge the same amount for two months plus, irrespective of the length of time spent abroad. On a long stay, this variation in the method of calculation produces a considerable difference in cost.

If there is a significant mis-match between your ideal

requirements and the cover on offer through your travel agent's standard policy, or if the premium is charged by the week from day one to the end, it will be worth your while to ask your bank, building society, the AA or the RAC for alternative quotations. Or you can consult an insurance broker, who will be able to arrange cover to suit your particular needs at a competitive rate.

You may already have an annual travel insurance policy. But beware – a number of firms which used to provide 91 days' continuous cover have now reduced it to 31 days at a stretch, though they may still provide 91 days' cover to long-established policy holders. Check your insurance certificate carefully and read the small print in the insurer's booklet. If your cover has been reduced, shop around. You will obviously use the 31 days' cover you have already paid for, but do not automatically extend it with your regular insurer. Another firm may offer better terms for the period beyond those 31 days.

TRAVEL INSURANCE FOR OLDER PEOPLE
If you are aged 65 or older, you may find that some insurers are reluctant to provide travel cover. The Norwich seem to be helpful towards this age group and Saga will provide cover for everyone travelling with them, irrespective of age. Contact the Help the Aged Senior Line (Tel: 0808 8006565) or the Age Concern Information Line (Tel: 0800 00 99 66) if you have problems.

5 LEGAL MATTERS

PASSPORTS
You should have the full standard ten-year passport for a winter abroad. Husbands and wives should have two separate passports for a number of reasons: in the course of a whole winter abroad, it might, for example, be necessary for one partner to make a flying visit home, while the other stayed behind; if any legal problems arose, necessitating the confiscation or retention of a passport by the authorities, it would be important for the other partner to have the protection of a passport and to be able to use it to prove British citizenship, if consular assistance were required; visas are generally issued only to full individual passport-holders.

If you do not already hold a full passport, please apply to the Passport Office early, as processing the application can take as much as two or three months during peak holiday periods. Application forms may be obtained from the Post Office.

If you already hold a full passport, check its expiry date. Some countries such as the United States, require the passport to be valid for a certain number of months, usually three or six, after the proposed date of departure from that country.

VISAS
Check any visa requirements with the travel agent who books your tickets. If in doubt, consult the Consulate of the country you intend to visit. Visas are not normally required for British citizens visiting Western Europe, but most other countries demand them and charge varying amounts of money to issue them. The requirements at the time of writing this handbook have been checked and are given in the Fact File under each country's entry in Part II. But regulations can change and it is better to double-check than to be grounded at Heathrow, or

refused entry to the country of your choice, because you have failed to fulfil the visa regulations.

Make a note of the number of your passport and the date and place of issue, and keep it separately. Do the same for any visa details. This will help speed up the issue of an emergency passport by the British Consul, should your current one be lost or stolen. It will also facilitate the re-issuing of a visa. Some people take photocopies of the vital pages, which is a good extra precaution.

DURATION OF VISIT

Many countries which do not require visas stipulate a maximum stay of ninety days. In the case of EC countries, where there is now freedom of movement and employment between member states, the ninety-day limit is probably just a piece of old legislation which has not yet been cleared from the statute books. As passports are no longer stamped at borders within the EC, it is difficult to see how a check can be kept. But it is better to keep within the letter of the law and arrange an official extension through the local authorities at the appropriate time, as detailed in Part II. In most cases it will be a mere formality. If you are within striking distance of a border, it is probably simpler to hop on a bus into the next country for the afternoon, before the expiry of the ninety days, and re-enter for a further ninety. Visas are issued for varying lengths of time (see the Fact File entries in Part II).

Please note: The requirements relating to passports, visas and duration of stay, which are given in this handbook, apply only to holders of full British Citizen passports, who are lawfully resident in the United Kingdom. The requirements for holders of British Dependent Territories passports, or British Overseas Citizen passports, may be different and must be checked with the appropriate Consulate, as must the requirements for holders of foreign passports.

LEGAL ASSISTANCE ABROAD

Laws vary from country to country, and so does the treatment of offenders. Do be sure that your documentation is in order, that you steer clear of drugs (trafficking carries the death penalty in some countries), that you do not infringe the local employment legislation (see below) and that you know the local laws in relation to motoring and alcohol. Ignorance of the law is no defence, either in England or abroad.

If, despite all precautions, you still run into legal difficulties, either as the offender or the offended, the British Consul is there to help you. The British Consul can:

provide a list of local lawyers, interpreters and doctors
visit you in prison
arrange for messages to be sent to family or friends
insist that you be treated as well as nationals of the country which is holding you.

The British Consul cannot:

give legal advice
instigate court proceedings on your behalf
interfere in local judicial procedures to get you out of prison
investigate a crime
pay for a lawyer
put up bail.

Generally speaking, the Consul will not give or loan money, though he may help to get it sent out to you, if you are in prison or hospital. He will not find you work or obtain a work permit for you, nor will he do any of the jobs which are more properly done by a travel agent, airline, bank or motoring association.

Loss or theft of passport The British Consul can issue an emergency passport. The procedure will be simpler and far more speedy if you can give full details of the number, date and place of issue of the old passport.

Theft in general   Report the loss first of all to the local police and obtain a statement from them. Then contact your insurance company, or carry out the instructions already given to policyholders. Contact the British Consul if you need a new passport, or any other emergency help. You are advised not to resist violent theft. It is better to lose your wallet than your life.

Death   Get in touch with the British Consul immediately. He will inform next of kin, if necessary, and advise on procedures.

A very useful leaflet, PU 2063 'Consular Assistance Abroad', prepared by the Central Office of Information for the Foreign and Commonwealth Office, is obtainable from most public libraries or direct from the COI (Tel: 020 7928 2345).

EMPLOYMENT LEGISLATION

As this book is not intended for those seeking regular, full-time work abroad, it is not the place for a detailed account of the relevant employment legislation. A general discussion can be found in a number of handbooks which deal specifically with employment overseas, and full details of the law as it applies to individual countries can be obtained from their Embassies or High Commissions in London. The observations in this chapter are intended for those who are going abroad for their own pleasure, not with the intention of working – but if the chance of a few hours' paid employment came their way, they would not necessarily turn it down.

AVAILABILITY OF WORK

The world is in economic recession and Britain is not the only country where jobs are hard to find. Vacancies in paid work are few and far between and employers will generally be obliged to give priority to local applicants. The notable exception is English-language teaching, where the demand for native speakers seems to be limitless. Most college proprietors will be looking for candidates with a University degree and/or a professional TEFL qualification (see p.23), but the market is expanding at such a rate that any articulate, confident English person may stand a chance of being taken on. Teaching experience helps, but it is not essential. Schools of English exist in almost every sizeable town abroad and they are worth approaching, as are local secondary schools. If you are looking for this kind of work, it is advisable to take your degree, TEFL or other professional qualification certificate with you.

Another area of employment is time-share or villa marketing, usually in resorts where many British families already own their own properties and the developers are anxious to add to their numbers from the pool of British holidaymakers. This work often involves aggressive 'hard sell' techniques and is not to everyone's taste.

If you speak the local language, there may also be a chance of some part-time bilingual secretarial or clerical work, particularly in travel agencies. Professionals with internationally needed skills, such as motor mechanics, clergymen, doctors or nurses, may also find some opportunities.

WORK PERMITS

Since the establishment of the single market, citizens of the EC no longer need work permits to take up paid employment in other member states. This relaxation of formalities is supposed to produce greater mobility of labour, but employment opportunities in Western Europe are at present so limited that it may be some time before there is in practice free movement across frontiers. If, however, you do manage to find employment, the law will probably allow you to take it up without a work permit. But do please check locally, to ensure that you are not contravening any regulations.

In almost all other countries, a work permit will be required before you take up paid employment. The permits are usually obtained on your behalf by the local employer, who has to demonstrate that no suitable national is available to fill the post.

In North America and Asia, it is very difficult indeed to acquire a permit. Australia is perhaps the easiest place to find casual work, though it is generally of the rough outdoor variety. Young people between 18 and 25 years may apply for a special one-year Australian Working Holiday Visa.

In some countries, it is illegal to enter as a tourist, look for a job and then apply for a permit. The job must be obtained and the work permit applied for in advance. In a few countries, retired foreigners are not allowed to work for pay.

In fact, the whole work permit situation is a minefield. If you are interested in the possibility of finding work, it is essential to contact the London Embassy or High Commission of the country of your choice before you leave home. You must be clear about the legislation and your information must be up to date. You should know whether you have to apply for a permit before leaving the UK, or whether you may apply for one locally. You should also know the penalties for working illegally – ejection from the country, a fine or imprisonment.

There are employers everywhere who are willing to contravene the regulations and offer a job without a work permit, but the very fact that they are prepared to break the law shows them to be unscrupulous or, at the very least, over-casual. They will not be the most reliable employers and you will have no redress if you have connived with them in breaking the law and are subsequently mistreated. So do make sure that the employer is applying on your behalf for any necessary permit, even if the work is only of a casual nature.

So what happens if you go abroad for the winter, with no intention of finding a job, and a local employer chances to offer you some really interesting work? If a work permit is necessary and the local legislation is such that your employer cannot take you on as a paid employee until he has gone through a lengthy application process, or until you have returned to the UK to get the necessary work permit from the Embassy here, you might consider offering your services free of charge for a few weeks. Then, if you found that you really enjoyed the work, you could arrange to go back the following winter, with all the necessary formalities completed, and take up the job as paid seasonal employment.

Sometimes it is better if no money changes hands. If you are interested in the possibility of teaching English, you can let it be known around the place that you are offering private English conversation lessons in exchange for lessons in the local language, or in exchange for coaching in tennis or golf, drawing lessons, violin lessons, or whatever you would like to have. No money will change hands, so that there will be no problems with income tax or work permits. Instead, you will have the opportunity to meet new people, visit them in their homes and make friends in the area. You will be performing a valuable and much appreciated service.

But before taking any job, do ask yourself if this is what you really want. Even the most casual work, once found, tends to snowball. A few extra hours are begged here, an extra commitment there, and in the end you may find yourself as busy and stress-ridden as you were in your full-time job at home, for much less than your previous remuneration. You retired or gave up your career after many years of relentless work. Now is your opportunity to relax in the sun and perhaps seek a new direction in your life. It would be a pity to be swept back into the rat race for the sake of a few pounds a week.

VOTING BY PROXY

If a general or local election is looming and you are keen to exercise your electoral rights, you should arrange a proxy vote. This can be done by contacting the Electoral Registration Office (usually to be found at the local Council Offices) and asking for application form RPF 11. If you do not have a suitable proxy to name on the form, contact the local office of your political party.

The agent is always keen to register votes and will arrange a proxy for you from amongst the local party workers.

WILLS AND WISHES

Whether you are at home or abroad, it is obviously wise to have a will and to update it from time to time to take account of changing circumstances. Your solicitor or executor probably has your will in safe keeping. When you go abroad for a long period, it is imperative to leave your affairs in good order, so that they can be dealt with easily in your absence. It is a good idea, in the course of tidying up, to make a list of your bank accounts, savings accounts, insurance policies, company shares and National Insurance number and to have this list stored with your will. Your executor will then be able to deal expeditiously with your estate. Your family and the person who is keeping an eye on your affairs during your absence should know where to find the will.

Before you leave home, make sure that your family, your closest friend or your solicitor is clear about your wishes, should you unfortunately die abroad. Depressing though it may be to talk about it, you should let your family know in advance whether you wish to be buried or cremated and whether you wish the arrangements to be made abroad or at home. It should be borne in mind that the cost of transporting a body is considerable, though ashes can, of course, be brought back home without particular difficulty or expense. If nothing but a home burial will do, you might consider taking out a special insurance policy to cover the costs.

6 LETTING AND INSURING YOUR HOME

TO LET OR NOT TO LET?

Everyone's circumstances are different and it would be inappropriate to attempt to give advice on such an individual matter. The decision on whether or not to let your own home must be a personal one. But it may be helpful to list the advantages and disadvantages of letting.

ADVANTAGES

1. Financial. You will be able to meet your mortgage payments and other standing charges from the rent of your property. If you have no mortgage, you may well be able to cover the entire cost of your winter abroad.
2. Security. Your home will be occupied and therefore less inviting to burglars, vandals and squatters.
3. Maintenance. Your property will be kept warm and in good running order throughout the winter. Emergency and routine repairs will be carried out and the garden kept tidy.

DISADVANTAGES

1. Effort. Setting up the arrangement involves a considerable amount of work and care.
2. Damage. Others will not care for your home as you do. Antique furniture is particularly vulnerable and you may either have to put it in store or have a special clause in the lease, prohibiting children and pets.
3. Non-availability. Should an emergency force you to return to the UK earlier than planned, it would be difficult, if not impossible, to terminate the tenancy before the date agreed in the lease.

Much will depend on the length of your absence. The longer the tenancy and the greater the financial benefit, the more worthwhile will be the effort and the risk.

If financial considerations are important to you, you may think that you have to let your home in order to go abroad. But life in a hotel in the sun *can* cost little more than the grocery bills at home, and you will be saving on heating, clothing and overheads. Choosing a cheaper resort, or a lower category hotel, could be as profitable in real terms as deriving an income from letting.

The final determinant may be whether or not you have a really comfortable alternative home, with family or friends, should you have to come back before the termination of the lease. Even the most healthy people can fall ill abroad, as I did once in India, and it is such a relief to be able to come back home and fall into your own bed, with your own doctor at hand.

LETTING YOUR HOME

Letting your home for the winter months is not as simple as it may at first appear. The Housing Act, 1988, was intended to encourage private rental by protecting the position of the landlord and simplifying letting procedures. But the legislation is still too complex for the layman to cope with satisfactorily and it is advisable to secure the services of an estate agent and/or solicitor.

LETTING THROUGH AN ESTATE AGENT

It is important to deal with an agent who has experience in property management as well as letting. He should be a member of the Royal Institute of Chartered Surveyors, the Incorporated Society of Valuers and Auctioneers, the Association of Residential Letting Agencies or the National Association of Estate Agents.

Most estate agents favour the Assured Shorthold Tenancy,

which runs for a minimum of six months. Some specialist agents arrange holiday lets by negotiating Assured Tenancies, usually for a maximum of three months, but the property needs to satisfy certain conditions as to location and the period during which it is available: it must be in the heart of London; near to a major sporting venue, such as Wimbledon or Goodwood, at the appropriate time of year; in a holiday area by the sea or the Scottish ski slopes and available during school holidays. Few people going abroad for the winter will have property which falls into one of these special categories. The majority will therefore need to arrange a six-month Assured Shorthold Tenancy. This is practicable only if you are planning to go away for the full six months, have family with whom you can spend a few weeks before or after your trip abroad, or are willing (and it is cost-effective) to stay in a hotel in England until the tenancy expires.

Agents' services, and the fees charged for them, vary somewhat from firm to firm, but market competition ensures that the variations are slight. The services offered are:

1. Introduction of the Tenant. This involves circulating details of the property, negotiating all terms and conditions of the proposed tenancy, taking up references on prospective tenants, preparing the tenancy agreement (the written contract between the landlord and tenant, which is both legally binding and enforceable), collecting the initial rental payment and deposit against damage, arranging for the preparation and checking of the landlord's inventory (this may be an additional charge) and notifying the utility companies of the change of subscriber. Most agencies charge 10 per cent of the rent payable for the term of the tenancy as their letting fee, plus VAT.

2. Rent Collection. For an extra 2½ per cent, or thereabouts, the agent will be responsible for the collection

of rent, will transfer the rent net of fees and VAT to the landlord's account and will submit a regular statement of account.

3. Comprehensive Management Services. In addition to collecting the rent, the agent will pay any regular outgoings chargeable to the landlord, such as ground rent and insurance premiums, will arrange for the day-to-day maintenance, repair and servicing of appliances, will inspect the property regularly and send a written report, check the inventory on the departure of the tenant and make a final inspection to ensure that the property is left clean and in good order. If necessary, cleaning contractors will be called in and their charges deducted from the tenant's deposit. The charge for these services, inclusive of the rent collection service, is usually 15 to 16 per cent of the rent collected, or a monthly sum based on the size of the property.

LETTING WITHOUT AN AGENT

It is, of course, possible to let your property through newspaper and magazine advertisements, or to friends or family. For periods of less than six months, these may in fact be your only options – but they are options which require particular care. Although you yourself will find the tenant, a solicitor should be involved in the drawing-up of the tenancy agreement.

The local estate agents are invaluable sources of information and advice. In the hope of getting your custom, they will gladly visit your property and advise you on the rent you should charge. They also produce extremely helpful booklets, detailing their services and giving general information on all aspects of letting, which will serve as check-lists for the arrangements which you yourselves will have to make.

A word of warning. Do not be tempted to let your property to embassy staff from overseas. They may appear to be charming and highly suitable tenants, but if they have Diplomatic Immunity, they are outside the jurisdiction of the British courts.

INSURANCE

It is advisable to inform your insurance company at an early stage of your intention to let your property, to ensure that you are not prejudicing your cover. Some insurance companies restrict the contents cover on tenanted property, while others increase the premium to cover the added risk. You should, in any case, consider putting any really valuable antique furniture or paintings in store and insuring them there.

It is also important to check that your policy covers you against third party claims, in case one of your tenants is injured through a faulty piece of equipment or a hole in the stair-carpet.

In addition, your estate agent or solicitor may advise you to arrange a letting protection policy. This will cover you against unpaid rents and pay the legal costs of eviction and also your hotel bills, should your tenant refuse to leave on the agreed date. Your right to repossession is protected by law, but a difficult tenant with a wily lawyer can cause considerable delay.

INCOME TAX

The rent from your property will count as unearned income and the profit you receive, after all deductible expenses, will be liable to UK income tax. Deductible expenses include:

agent's fees, including VAT
insurance of property and contents
postage and telephone costs relating to the letting
legal fees and accountancy charges
water rates
ground rent

repairs, maintenance and re-decoration, but not
   improvements
cleaning, including window-cleaning
gardening costs
TV rental
your own rent, if you do not own the property
depreciation of furniture and fittings (the practice of the
   Inland Revenue is to allow 10 per cent of the gross rent
   for wear and tear).

COUNCIL TAX

This tax, which came into effect on 1 April 1993, is regarded as
a charge on the tenants and their responsibility for paying it is
made clear in most tenancy agreements.

MORTGAGES

Mortgage interest is not normally an allowable expense.

You will need to seek approval from your building society or
bank, if you are proposing to let the property. Approval is
normally given on payment of a small fee for issuing a letter of
authority to sub-let.

TENANCIES

If you yourself are a tenant, it is important to check your lease to
ensure that it does not contain a covenant prohibiting sub-
letting. You may be required to inform your landlord, even if
letting is permitted. If in doubt, check the position with your
solicitor.

As the whole rental process, from the initial contacts to the
signing of the tenancy agreement, can take anything up to two
months, it is important to set the proceedings in motion at least
three months before departure. A suitable tenant is sometimes
slow to appear.

An Inland Revenue booklet, IR 87 'Rooms to Let. Income

from Letting Property' is available from your local Tax Office. Despite the reference to rooms in the title, the booklet does deal with the letting of whole houses too and is full of useful information. Your Tax Inspector will help you with any special queries.

LEAVING YOUR HOME UNOCCUPIED
If you are leaving your home unoccupied, you must obviously take all possible steps to keep it secure.

SAFETY MEASURES

1. Inform the police of your absence, so that they may keep a special eye on your property. Give them the name and telephone number of your designated contact.
2. Ask the neighbours to be on the alert. If there is a local branch of Neighbourhood Watch, inform the organizer.
3. Pay a local person to keep the garden tidy.
4. Leave jewellery, silver and other small valuables in a safe-deposit box at your bank.
5. Consider putting any valuable furniture, pictures or porcelain into storage and insuring it there.
6. Turn off main services.
7. Be sure to cancel milk, newspapers and other deliveries. Arrange for the collection or redirection of mail.

A few residential letting agencies are prepared to offer management and supervisory services, even if the property is unlet.

INSURANCE
Most domestic policies cover the house and its contents if it is occupied by the policy holder. If you read the small print in your policy, you will probably find that cover lapses if your home is left unoccupied for more than thirty days. There are two

solutions to this problem. One is to inform the insurers and pay the extra premium on a vacant property. The other is to arrange for a member of your family, or the friend who picks up your post, to spend a night or two in your home within each month.

In addition, someone needs to look in on a regular basis, as it is vital to inform the insurers immediately any damage occurs. If, for instance, vandals were to break into your home, and there were then to be a second break-in through the point of entry created by the first intruders, you would not be covered for the damage caused in the second incident, if the insurance company had not already been informed of the first. In a similar way, if storm damage to the roof or a burst pipe were not reported promptly, you would not be covered for the continuing damage caused by delay in reporting and repair.

OTHER OPTIONS

If you are not arranging an official let of your home, but are unhappy at the idea of leaving it vacant, there are a few other options.

There might be a young member of your family, a recently widowed aunt, or a close friend who is job-hunting in the area, who would be delighted to have the use of your home for a few months. You might charge a token rent, or simply arrange for the tenant to pay the domestic bills. You would be doing someone a good turn, protecting your property from break-ins and at least covering your running costs. But even though this sort of arrangement is unofficial, it is essential to set down clearly the terms and conditions upon which you are making your home available, so that there will be no misunderstandings. It is wise to have the terms checked by a solicitor.

If you have no suitable candidate for this house-sitting among your own intimate circle, agencies such as Absentia Limited, Little London, Berden, Bishop's Stortford, Herts. CM23 1BE, Tel: (01279) 777412, Universal Aunts Limited, 19 The Chase, London SW4 0NP, Tel: 0207 738 8937, or www.home-and-pets.co.uk will provide reliable people, with good references, to live in and look after your house, garden and pets, answer the telephone and take messages. The agency will be responsible for the protection of your property, but you will have to pay dearly for the service. Absentia, for example, currently charges £27.50 plus VAT a day, depending on the number of pets to be cared for. In addition, there is board of £6.00 a day for the house-watcher, plus travel expenses. An agency house-sitter is therefore a very expensive option.

Writers sometimes advertise in literary magazines for a quiet place to work on a book in return for house-sitting duties and the *Lady* magazine is a good source of unofficial female house-sitters, whose terms are considerably less exacting than the terms of those supplied by agencies. It is a good idea to place an advertisement in one of those periodicals, or in limited-circulation special-interest magazines. Be sure to give a Box Number, otherwise you will be giving very convenient information to burglars!

It is prudent to discuss the arrangements with your solicitor and to take up references before you leave your home in the care of a stranger.

7 YOUR CAR

Some people are addictive drivers and are never happy without their steel carapace and their hands on a steering wheel. If you belong to that category, you will choose a resort which you can reach by land and ferry and make the journey out and back enjoyable parts of your winter abroad. Other people regard their cars as a necessary evil, a means of getting from A to B and a cheap way to transport a family. For most, the decision on whether or not to take the car will be an easy one. But if in doubt, don't! Public transport in a foreign country is an experience in itself and a good way to meet the locals. Taxis are often cheaper abroad than they are at home; and you can always hire a car or a moped for a special trip.

TAKING YOUR CAR WITH YOU
If you really want to take your car with you, your insurers and your motoring organization will help you with the necessary documentation.

INSURANCE
Until recently, your insurer would issue you with a Green Card International Insurance carnet, endorsed for the countries through which you intended to travel. But in recent years, this practice has been dropped in favour of a chit from your insurer.

Most countries have insurance agencies at their frontier posts, where the proper insurance may be purchased. This can be very useful if you wish to add an extra country to your itinerary, or if you have made a vital omission.

DRIVING LICENCES
It is an offence to drive a vehicle in any country without a valid driving licence or permit. When you have decided on your

winter destination, please check with the AA or RAC, who will be able to tell you the current licence requirements.

The new pink UK driving licence is accepted throughout Western Europe, but holders of the old green licence have to obtain translations for use in some countries. It is probably easier to change your green licence to a pink one, using form D1 from the Post Office.

For countries outside Western Europe, an International Driving Permit is either obligatory or recommended. There are two kinds. Normally, the 1949 permit will be issued, but for certain countries the 1926 Convention permit is required. The AA and RAC will issue the appropriate application forms over the counter in their shops, or through the post. The permits cost £3 each and each application must be accompanied by a passport-size photograph, signed on the back.

These International Driving Permits normally allow the holder to drive a private motor vehicle without further formality. They are issued only to permanent residents over the age of eighteen, who hold a full driving licence; and they must be obtained before you leave the UK, as they are invalid in their country of issue. It is important to find out from the AA or RAC how long the International Driving Permit is valid in your chosen country (usually one year) before you need to take a local test, and where you may renew it if no test is required.

The application form lists all the countries for which the two types of permit are required or recommended. If in doubt, it is better to be on the safe side and obtain the appropriate International Driving Permit.

All drivers are recommended to carry their own British driving licence as well as their International Driving Permit. This is especially important if you are thinking of hiring cars, as some car rental firms abroad insist on seeing the national driving licence too.

OTHER DOCUMENTATION
You must always carry your car's registration book and insurance documents. The AA and RAC will be able to inform you of any other documents which are required or advisable for the countries you are visiting.

TOURING AND AUTOMOBILE CLUBS
If you belong to the AA or RAC, ask them about reciprocal arrangements with touring clubs abroad. Most national clubs are affiliated to the International Touring Alliance in Geneva and extend their services to one another's members. You may find that you are entitled to useful assistance from the Touring and Automobile Club in your winter destination through your membership of the AA or RAC in Britain. The national tourist office of your chosen country in London will be able to give you the address and emergency telephone numbers of their Touring and Automobile Club. It might also be useful to get the same information from the tourist offices of the countries you will be crossing on the way to your destination.

DURATION OF STAY
Some countries set a maximum of three months as the period during which a tourist may keep an imported car there. It is usually possible to extend the period by applying to the local Touring and Automobile Club for a triptique; or you can simply drive your car on a short visit to a neighbouring country, then re-import it for a further three months. If you are quite near to a border, that is by far the simplest course. Again, the British motoring organizations should be able to advise you. If in doubt, check with the consulate or tourist office of your chosen country before leaving home.

SERVICE FACILITIES
Before deciding to take your own car abroad for a number of months, do find out if there are service facilities for your particular make and model within reasonable distance. Your

dealers' handbook may list overseas garages. If not, you should write to the manufacturer. You will have little difficulty with repairs to popular models in Western Europe. But although mechanics elsewhere may be brilliant at keeping cars going on string and chewing gum, that may not be the healthiest course for your engine!

Most owners treat their cars to a major service before embarking on a long trip abroad. They then hope to be able to manage without mechanical assistance until their return. But unless you are a skilful mechanic yourself, it is as well to make sure that expert help and recognized spare parts are available locally in an emergency, before you drive off in your car to parts of North Africa, for instance. If they are not, it would be better not to risk taking it.

LUGGAGE AND CAR RADIOS

Although it may be the last thing you feel like doing at the end of a long day's drive, it pays to unload your car completely every single night – not only the suitcases, but the car radio, if it is detachable, the documents from the glove compartment and any sports equipment. Many travellers have had their holidays ruined by the theft of their belongings on the journey out and it is worth taking that extra bit of trouble.

LEAVING YOUR CAR BEHIND

GARAGING

For those with a lockable garage, this is no problem. But if you do not have your own garage, you will need to beg, borrow or rent one, or at the very least arrange secure parking. It would obviously be an open invitation to theft to leave your car unused in the road for such a long period and it would not please the local police.

MAINTENANCE

If you are handy with cars, you will know exactly what needs to be done to prevent your own car from deteriorating during your absence. But if you are among the majority, who are quite good at driving but know nothing of what goes on under the bonnet, you will need to consult your garage, and possibly get one of the mechanics to come round and prepare your car for its hibernation. You will certainly be advised to remove the battery and the garage may have useful suggestions to help preserve the bodywork and the tyres.

INSURANCE

If your car is off the road in a securely locked garage, you will be able to make substantial savings by converting your vehicle insurance cover from an 'on road' to a 'laid up' policy. Your car will then be insured during your absence only against accidental damage, fire and theft. Your car insurance firm will be able to quote for this limited cover. If your house contents are insured by a different firm, it would be worth your while to ask them to quote for the inclusion of your off-road car under your domestic cover. You could then compare the two quotations and possibly insure the car at a lower rate.

VEHICLE LICENCE

Your car will not need to have a road licence if it is locked up in your garage, but you must complete the S.O.R.N. (Statutory Off Road Notification) on your tax renewal reminder V11.

FAMILY USE

If your car is an old friend rather than a shiny new toy, why not let a member of your family, or a friend without a car, have the use of it and incur all expenses during your absence? It would save you trouble, as well as money.

OTHER STRATEGIES

BUYING ABROAD FOR RE-SALE

We in England are used to right-hand drive, but a few hours at the wheel of a left-hand drive car will be enough to demonstrate its advantages in countries where traffic flows down the right-hand side. The nervous tension and actual danger of overtaking in a right-hand drive car will be eliminated and you will soon feel so comfortable that you will forget you ever drove on the other side. So if you decide that you really need a car throughout your winter escape and will not be content with the occasional day's hire, there is something to be said for buying a second-hand car shortly after your arrival, with the intention of selling it again before you return home. This is particularly easy to arrange in the United States and Australia, where second-hand cars are plentiful and relatively inexpensive. The cost of purchase might be considerably less than a long-term hire arrangement.

Another major advantage of this option over taking your own car is the freedom from red tape. Insurance and vehicle tax are arranged locally by the people who know all about it, there are no import and export formalities and everything can be finalized swiftly and easily.

You may also find that your running costs are considerably less. Check the relative prices of petrol (leaded and unleaded) and diesel before you go to the dealers. In some countries, diesel can cost as little as half the price of petrol. In others, leaded fuel is no longer available. The cheapness and availability of the fuel required to run the car will obviously have a significant influence on your choice.

Finally, if your car is bought locally, you will be able to get it repaired without difficulty, possibly even under guarantee.

BUYING ABROAD FOR IMPORT

If you are thinking of buying a new car in any case, there may be advantages in an overseas purchase. In areas where there are many resident British, such as the South of France, the local dealers even stock right-hand drive vehicles. Elsewhere, right-hand drive cars may be specially ordered.

Dealers' margins on the Continent are often lower than the margins of British dealers, so that the identical model may cost substantially less abroad than it does at home. In addition, there may be some savings on VAT. The subject is much too complicated to come within the scope of this handbook. It requires exhaustive research into specific models, their purchase price in individual countries, the rate of VAT applied to purchases there and the length of time the car is to be used abroad before it is imported. Travellers who are interested in this possibility should approach the British manufacturer, or the sole selling agent of a foreign manufacturer in the United Kingdom, for details of the import regulations applying to their models purchased overseas. They should then research the comparative retail prices of the models which interest them in the countries they may be visiting. It is a project for those who enjoy a challenge!

There are firms which specialize in importing UK specification vehicles from the Continent at anything from a 2 per cent to 23 per cent saving on UK prices, and some of these firms will reduce the price even further if you collect your new car from the dealer yourself. As with any major purchase, you should take all the necessary precautions:

(a) Make sure the company has a land line, not just a mobile number.

(b) Make sure they publish their business address.

(c) Get a written quotation.

(d) Pay no money upfront, except perhaps a dealer's deposit.

(e) Pay by credit card for that little extra security.

SELLING BEFORE YOU GO

If the time has come for a trade-in of your present model, you could hand it over to your motor dealer before you go and arrange to take delivery of your new car immediately on your return. This will save the expense and trouble of its upkeep during your absence. The time-lag between relinquishing your old model and taking delivery of your new one will also be a useful bargaining counter in your negotiations with your dealer. Your dealer should either pay you on the spot for your old model, so that the proceeds can earn interest in a deposit account during your absence, or he should make an extra deduction from the price of the new model to compensate for your loss of income. He will be having the use of your money throughout the winter and must expect to pay for it.

I know from my own experience that this is a very simple and cost-effective arrangement. It is such a relief, and a saving, to be rid of the responsibility for the old car during the winter, and having a new car to look forward to has helped to make coming home an excitement rather than an anticlimax.

NOTES FOR ALL DRIVERS

DOCUMENTATION

Most drivers like to feel that the use of a car is available to them. So whether you decide to take your own car abroad, buy one out there, or manage with the occasional hire, you will need to ensure that you have a driving licence with you, which is legally valid for your chosen country (see above). Your driving licence(s), insurance policy and passport should be carried at all times when you travel by car. The police in some countries are very fond of spot checks and having the correct documentation to hand is a great help.

TRAFFIC FLOW

When everyone drives on 'the wrong side of the road', you will automatically follow them and the direction of the traffic-flow will soon seem to be perfectly normal. But do take extra care on empty roads. I have almost met with disaster on a few occasions, when I have driven out of a filling-station on to a clear road and absent-mindedly accelerated up the left-hand lane. The sight of an oncoming lorry has woken me up sharply!

A LAST WORD

I am sure that none of you drink and drive. But, even so, make sure that you know the local regulations, as penalties in some countries are very severe. And beware of that cheap local brandy. It can be lethal – literally!

8 MEDICAL MATTERS

Health warning Reading this chapter will be like reading a book of medical symptoms. Even the fittest will turn pale at the thought of all the dire diseases which may strike abroad. But take heart! The great majority of people who escape the winter not only stay well, but return home positively glowing after months of sunshine, good food and stress-free living. But even heaven on earth can be ruined by toothache or diarrhoea, so it is important to take all possible steps to ensure your good health whilst abroad.

BEFORE YOU GO

THE DOCTOR
At least two months before you go, arrange a consultation with your doctor. You may need a general check-up and you will certainly have to plan the spacing-out of any inoculations.

INOCULATIONS
The basics Wherever you are going, make sure that you still have protection from tetanus. And if you are under sixty and have not had polio vaccine for many years, it is worth asking the doctor for a booster. Polio may have died out in Britain, but it is still a crippler in some countries overseas.
Special requirements Your doctor will be able to advise you on any specific inoculations needed for your own winter destination. Some are given on an NHS prescription, while the more exotic ones have to be paid for. When you have been inoculated, be sure to take the relevant certificates with you.

MALARIA PROPHYLAXIS
If you are going to a country where malaria is prevalent, it is essential to get the latest malaria guidelines from the experts, as

there are different strains of the disease and some mosquitos have become resistant to some anti-malarial drugs. You should consult:

MASTA (The Medical Advisory Service for Travellers Abroad)
London School of Hygiene and Tropical Medicine
Keppel Street
London WC1E 7BR
Tel: (020) 7636 7921 www.masta.org

Liverpool School of Tropical Medicine
Pembroke Place
Liverpool L3 5QA
Tel: (0151) 708 9393

Large travel firms, such as British Airways, Thomas Cook and Trailfinders, also have specialist clinics in London, which give up-to-date advice, sell the tablets and have an inoculation service. www.netdoctor.co.uk/travel is a useful site to visit.

ROUTINE MEDICATION

Travellers who are normally on medication of any kind should take a large enough supply to last throughout their stay abroad. The drugs may well be available over the counter in the local pharmacy, but travelling with your own stock is simpler. It may also save money, as drugs abroad can be expensive. Ask your doctor for the generic name of the drugs as well as their brand names, so that the local chemist can supply the equivalent, if you run out and your own brand is not available. Other useful prescription drugs, which your doctor may recommend are:

a course of wide-spectrum antibiotics
a pack of tablets to calm diarrhoea (codeine phosphates, loperamides or diphenoxylates)

a penicillin powder (such as Cicatrin) to puff on to troublesome cuts or grazes.

It is useful to prepare a small first-aid pack of your own favourite patent remedies, such as laxatives, indigestion tablets, headache remedies, throat pastilles, antiseptic cream, plasters, rubs for aching joints, insect repellent and antihistamine cream. Take a modest amount of each and keep them in their packets. If you run out, the local pharmacist will then be able to match the ingredients and give you the local equivalent, if not the very same brand.

WATER PURIFICATION

A small pack of Puritabs or the more expensive Swiss Micropur MTI tablets is a good idea, as you may go on an excursion where the cleanliness of the water is in doubt and no bottled water is available. Be sure to get the tablets which treat water in small quantities, not in gallons at a time.

STERILE EQUIPMENT

AIDS can be transmitted by used needles. If you like to be on the safe side, you can take your own sterile needles, in case injections are needed. Complete sterile medical equipment packs, produced by MASTA and Lifesystems, are on sale in larger pharmacies at prices ranging from £16.99 to £29.99, depending on contents. Make sure that these packs are clearly marked 'First Aid', or you may be hauled in by Customs on suspicion of drug addiction! Single needles are also available. The alternative to taking your own supplies from home is to watch the local practitioner like a hawk and refuse to have any injection from a used needle. Sterile ones will be on sale in the local pharmacies.

Condoms are available worldwide.

THE DENTIST

A dental check-up before you leave is another essential. As appointments for non-emergencies sometimes involve a long wait, it is important to go for the preliminary check-up at least two months ahead of departure, to allow time for any necessary treatment. If you have been 'waiting to see' about a dubious tooth, wait no longer. A broken crown or a lost filling will be much more difficult to deal with abroad, where you may have to scour the district for a recommended English-speaking dentist.

People with real problem teeth should ask their dentist for an emergency travel pack, which will include a do-it-yourself temporary filling kit, adhesive for dislodged crowns and a sterile needle, together with instructions on their use. These packs are produced by MASTA and Lifesystems and can also be bought in pharmacies for £8.99.

MEDICAL TREATMENT ABROAD

Medical treatment on the spot is sometimes necessary. For minor ailments, the pharmacist is consulted much more often abroad than is generally the case at home, so the local chemist's shop is the place to go first about a persistent cough or an upset stomach. Pharmacists usually speak English and sign language is in any case highly effective.

RECIPROCAL ARRANGEMENTS FOR TREATMENT

If you are very unlucky, you may need to visit a doctor abroad or even go into hospital. Travellers to an EC country are entitled to receive the same free or reduced-price medical treatment as the citizens of that country, under the terms of reciprocal agreements between the United Kingdom and other member states. To qualify for this treatment, you must obtain Form E111 (E-one-eleven) before leaving home. You may or may not have to pay for the treatment at the time and reclaim the money afterwards. Details of the arrangements, together with the appropriate application form, are given in Leaflet T6 'Health Advice for

Travellers', which may be obtained from any post office. This booklet contains a useful check-list for inoculations.

PRIVATE HEALTH INSURANCE

Despite the criticisms levelled against it, the British National Health Service is the envy of the world and the State treatment you would receive abroad would probably be well below the standard you have come to expect at home. Whether you are travelling in the EC or beyond, there is no substitute for comprehensive medical insurance to cover the cost of private treatment. I have travelled in some very difficult parts of the world and it has always been of immeasurable comfort to know that I have even been covered for helicopters and air-ambulances home, should a really urgent problem arise. Medical cover is the most important part of your travel insurance and you should never skimp on it.

The range of medical cover is wide. £250,000 for Europe is the minimum you should consider, while £2 million is not too much to contemplate for the East, or the United States, where medical costs are devastatingly high. Your general state of health is, of course, a factor to be taken into account. Read the small print carefully, to ensure that you are not excluded on grounds of age, pregnancy or medical condition, and that you are covered for any sporting activities you may wish to undertake. If you are hoping to find casual employment abroad, check up on the cover you have for accidents whilst working.

Your policy and the accompanying documents will tell you how to call for help in emergencies. You may have to pay for treatment on the spot and reclaim later, so make sure that you have access to sufficient funds (see Chapter 4) and that you obtain receipts for everything you pay, from the cost of bone-setting to taxi rides to the hospital. If you are on a long-stay winter package, the local representatives will be able to help in an emergency.

Some private health-care firms have now entered the travel

insurance market with schemes such as BUPA Travel and the PPP Travel Plan, both of which offer comprehensive protection to their members.

KEEPING WELL ABROAD

If you are spending the winter in one place, you will be less prone to travellers' illnesses than those who are constantly on the move. You will have the leisure to shop with care and pack your own picnics; there will be none of those hurried snacks, seized from dubious railway stalls, which are often the start of Montezuma's Revenge. Nor will you have to exhaust yourselves by rushing off to keep appointments the minute the plane lands; you can let your body recover from the journey in its own time.

JET LAG

This is not a minor discomfort, to be disregarded, but a real problem. Some researchers have estimated that it takes a day to adjust to every time zone crossed. So if, for instance, your destination has a time difference of four hours from home, you will need roughly four days to recover fully. In the meantime, you may suffer from fatigue, lack of concentration, disruption of sleeping and eating patterns and general disorientation. It is important to get plenty of rest and, above all, to avoid taking major decisions during the first few days. Avoiding alcohol, taking off your shoes and using an inflatable neck-pillow on a long flight will all help to mitigate the effects.

ACCLIMATIZATION

How quickly you adjust will obviously depend on the temperature difference between home and your resort. But if at first you take it easy, increase your liquid intake to avoid dehydration and wear loose clothing, you will speed up the process and will soon feel comfortable and relaxed.

Remember that alcohol dehydrates and go steady for the first few days.

If you are spending the winter in a substantially hotter climate, you will find that salt, taken in tablet form or as a little extra sprinkled on your food, will help to prevent dehydration. But you must, of course, consult your doctor if you are on a low salt diet for medical reasons.

STOMACH TROUBLE

This has ruined many holidays, but a few sensible precautions will help to prevent it. Most of the traditional winter destinations have tap water which is safe to drink and restaurants which are every bit as clean as those in Britain. If you get a touch of diarrhoea, it is more likely to be caused by a change in the composition of the water, or by unfamiliar ingredients in the cooking, than by lack of hygiene. It will soon pass.

In more exotic locations (and perhaps for the first couple of weeks in any strange environment):

Do not
    eat uncooked foods, such as salads, unless you are
      confident that they have been washed in clean water
    eat cooked food which has been on display for a long
      time
    eat any food which has flies or insects on it
    drink tap water, unless you know that it has been
      treated
    clean your teeth with tap water
    have ice cubes in your drinks

Be wary of
    shellfish
    ice cream

Do

    drink boiled or bottled water, or treat other water with
      Puritabs

    make sure that the milk is pasteurized or boiled

    peel all fruit, unless you have washed it yourself in
      good water.

Little by little, most people acquire some immunity to local bacteria, but you will know from experience how delicate your own system is and how quickly you can start to take a few risks – if ever.

If you *are* afflicted, despite all reasonable precautions, do not rush to the medicine kit. Unlike the roving traveller, you have a comfortable bed and the time to let your body cope on its own. This is the ideal solution to the problem, as you will build up immunity against recurrences. Medical advice is to rest as much as possible, eat lightly and drink far more than usual, to prevent dehydration (hot, weak black tea is particularly recommended).

Drugs such as Lomotil or Imodium should be taken only if you have to travel during an attack. Their function is simply to calm the intestines and alleviate cramps and frequency; they do nothing to cure the problem. Antibiotics are even worse, as they kill off the benign organisms in the digestive system as well as the harmful ones and leave it less resistant to future infection. Those who are ill abroad with great frequency are generally those who have overdosed themselves on modern drugs.

Diarrhoea and/or vomiting should pass within three days. If it lasts longer, if there is blood or pus, or if you have a persistent high temperature, you should consult a doctor.

MALARIA

If you are going to a country where malaria is prevalent, you should start taking your anti-malaria tablets a week before departure and continue with them for four weeks after your return, as the incubation period of the parasite in the liver is ten to twenty days.

Hotels without air conditioning usually provide mosquito nets, electric devices with insecticide mats or mosquito coils, and all these are available in local shops. As evenings are peak biting times, be sure to wear long trousers and long sleeves when you go out to dinner, and use mosquito repellent. One of the delights of the tropics is dining out under the stars – but you may need to take your own mosquito coil and have it smouldering under the table. The best anti-malarial precaution is to avoid getting bitten.

A small tip: anti-malaria tablets are hard on even the strongest stomachs. At one time, I took them with my breakfast and felt slightly sick all morning. Then I discovered, quite by chance, that if I took them at bedtime, after my main meal of the day, I suffered no discomfort at all.

AIDS

AIDS does not go away because you are on holiday abroad. The disease is spread by sexual contact with an infected person, transfusions of contaminated blood and injections with contaminated needles. You should obviously be as prudent and vigilant abroad as you are at home.

THE SUN

If you are going to be abroad in the sun for a number of months, you are less likely to be afflicted by sunburn or sunstroke than those on a fortnight's holiday, who may be tempted to spend every moment baking on the beach. You will be able to acquire an enviable tan gradually, with no damage to the skin, if you begin with fifteen to twenty minutes' sunbathing a day and use a sun-cream of the appropriate factor for your skin. Fortunately for the delicate, the increase in skin cancer has lessened the popularity of the bronzed, outdoor look, and pale is now cool.

Be particularly careful if you are going to the southern hemisphere, as it will be high summer there.

If my own experience is anything to go by, you are unlikely to suffer anything worse than a cold in the head. But precautions, like umbrellas, are negative magic. If you take them, your health will stay as fine as the weather.

9 PACKING

I should not presume to make a list of the clothes you should pack for your winter abroad. That is a matter of style and taste and is only partly influenced by the climate. I shall just make four general points:

1. Light clothing, which can be worn in layers, is by far the most useful. You will get much more wear, and a more varied wardrobe, out of two lightweight jerseys, which can be worn separately or together depending on the temperature, than you will out of one bulky winter-weight woolly.

2. Life abroad in the sun tends to be more relaxed and clothing consequently less formal. Two smart outfits will be ample for the independent traveller. Those on a winter package in a smart hotel, where dinner and evening entertainments are included, may wish to take several changes of formal wear. For men, a blazer is a very useful garment, as it can be dressed up for evening as well as being suitable for sports wear – unlike a sports jacket.

3. Shorts are not appreciated in Muslim countries, or in the more conservative Roman Catholic and Greek Orthodox communities, except on the beach. Be sure to take long-sleeved shirts or blouses for visiting churches and mosques.

4. If in doubt about an item of clothing, leave it behind. There is no country on earth where an extra shirt, blouse or pair of socks cannot be purchased. And shopping for a few cheap and cheerful local garments can add to the fun. They can always be left behind at the end of the season. In poorer countries, where everything is put to good use, your cleaner will seize upon your cast-offs with warm appreciation.

The following is a list of items, other than clothes and medicines (see Chapter 8), which I have found to be extremely useful, if not essential, on long stays abroad:

- A small electric kettle with adaptor and a modest starter pack of instant coffee and teabags
- A Swiss Army knife, with bottle-opener, corkscrew, scissors, etc.
- A universal plug for washbasins and baths
- A small nylon rucksack for walks, overnight stays and for use on the journeys out and back
- A transistor radio, capable of receiving BBC World Service broadcasts on short wave
- Maps of the country and area (good ones are not always easy to find locally)
- A phrase book and small pocket dictionary (Langenscheidt or Collins Gem)
- Two really solid books (history, poetry etc.), which will merit re-reading if English books are hard to find in local shops
- Playing cards, set for one game – e.g. chess, backgammon or scrabble
- Books of crosswords or logic puzzles (long-lasting entertainment in relation to their weight)
- A torch
- Extra visa photographs
- Degree certificate or other professional qualification and copies of c.v., if work is to be sought
- Snaps of family, home and home town, for social use
- One or two family photographs, or a few small cherished knick-knacks, to make you feel at home
- A stock of small gifts (biros, sweets, postcards, cigarettes) and one or two specially English gifts for your hostess, in case you are invited out to a meal or to stay (soaps, small china items, gift-packaged jams and marmalades, a

Liberty scarf – all things which you can enjoy yourselves
if they are not needed!)
Golf clubs, if really keen (most courses hire out clubs to the
occasional player), or tennis raquets.

Clothes can be bought anywhere, but the above items are
sometimes difficult to obtain abroad and are well worth their
weight and space in the suitcase. Remember the baggage
allowance on a scheduled flight is twenty kilograms and may be
less on budget airlines.

It is wise to make your luggage list well in advance and add
to it as items come to mind. I find it a good discipline to lay out
all the listed items on a spare-room bed, as soon as they are ready
for packing. I am usually so horrified at the size of the growing
mountain that I prune my original list drastically!

10 LIFESTYLE

SETTLING IN

Once you have decided on your hotel, your first thought will obviously be to telephone to your nominated contact and the members of your family to give them your telephone number and full postal address. Do it on the hotel phone or on your mobile, if you can't wait. If you can exercise a little patience, it is much cheaper to go to the Post Office or telephone centre and come to grips with the public telephone system. Most countries these days have phone cards and international direct dialling and you will find it quite simple to phone home, once you have learned the ropes.

INITIAL SUPPLIES

After unpacking and setting out your books and photographs, you will need to go shopping:

> One cheap knife, fork, spoon, plate, mug, glass per person for picnic lunches or suppers
> A bottle or two, plus nuts, crisps, olives, to set up your own bar
> A supply of fruit
> Perhaps a pot plant or a bunch of flowers.

Those choosing self-catering accommodation will of course need to shop for basic foodstuffs, but not for the crockery and cutlery.

SAFEKEEPING

It is important to make an early decision on the safekeeping of money, valuables and passport. They should either be handed in at Reception against a receipt, to be kept in the hotel safe, or preserved with the utmost care. If you decide to keep them in your own possession, divide them up between various pockets or money-belts on your own person and various unlikely receptacles in locked suitcases. Except in some South American countries, theft abroad is no more of a problem than it is at home, but it is as well to be prudent. Keeping all your worldly goods in one pocket, wallet or drawer makes life much too easy for the criminal and could deprive you of everything essential in one fell swoop. Remember that most thieves are opportunists. If they find an unlocked receptacle, they will steal its contents, but they will rarely stop to pick the lock on the off-chance that they may find something valuable inside. I find it useful to make a cryptic note in my diary of what I have stowed away where. Otherwise I spend hours turning out sponge-bags and medicine-kits, searching for traveller's cheques which I have hidden too well! I always feel safer if I have my passport on my own person at all times. Passports, with their accompanying visas, are vital documents and should never be handed over to other people, unless their credentials are absolutely certain.

EMERGENCY ADDRESSES

If you are not on a long-stay package with a tour operator, where there will probably be a company representative to cope with any emergencies, it is a good idea to find the name, address and telephone number of a reputable English-speaking doctor and dentist early in your stay. With luck, you will not need the services of either, but it is a great comfort to have the information handy. I know myself from a bad experience in New York how frightening it can be to have a medical emergency in a hotel in the middle of the night. Fortunately, I was in an English-speaking country and Reception were efficient. But it taught me a lesson: never wait until the emergency occurs before finding out where to get help. The hotel receptionist, the local tourist office or, failing them, the local pharmacy should be able to supply the information you need. You might at the same time find out the address and telephone number of the nearest British Consul, if you do not have the information already.

TELEVISION AND RADIO

You will probably have a television set in your hotel room. If you are lucky, you will be able to receive BBC World, Sky and CNN. If you are unlucky, you will have an old-fashioned set, and all your programmes will be terrestrial, in the local language. The news will reflect local preoccupations and viewpoints and you will miss your normal perspective on world events, even though you may be able to follow the Spanish or Turkish quite well. To get round the problem, ask the management if the hotel has a satellite dish. If it does, you can probably arrange to hire a suitable television for the duration of your stay. If not, you will just have to make friends with residents in more plush hotels and watch your favourite programmes on their sets!

To receive the BBC World Service on the radio, take a small Roberts or Sony or similar, capable of receiving short-wave broadcasts. There are plenty on the market and they are not expensive.

The BBC publishes a highly readable monthly magazine, *On Air*, priced at £2, which gives programmes for overseas television and radio. If you do not wish to take out a subscription, at least buy one copy, as 'London Calling', the pull-out centre section of the magazine, contains all the radio frequencies for the BBC World Service and a month's radio and television programmes. It will give you the information you need to tune in your radio and will be a useful guide to the times of news broadcasts, current affairs programmes and other regular features. You can have it posted out to you by paying an annual subscription. Contact BBC *On Air*, BBC World Service, Bush House, Strand, London WC2B 4PH.

KEEPING IN TOUCH WITH HOME

MOBILE PHONES

You may like to take your mobile phone with you. Before you go, check with the phone user's manual and with the service provider for any limitations or special requirements for making calls to the UK from abroad. Your provider will be able to inform you if your dual-band phone can be used in your chosen country. A tri-band phone will be needed for the USA. It is possible to hire one in this country or in the States. Remember to take your phone charger and a travel plug adaptor with you.

Warning! When someone at home phones you on your mobile abroad, there is a double charge. The caller pays to make the call and you pay to receive it. This is because the amount paid by the caller does not include the cost of making the international link. Mobile phones are strictly for emergency use only.

For incoming calls, it is much cheaper for both parties, and just as convenient, if your family and friends call you on your hotel phone. For outgoing calls, a long chat in the comfort of your hotel room may seem attractive, but you will pay heavily for it, as hotels always pile on the charges. It is far cheaper to buy a phonecard and use a public call box, or one of the metered phones in post offices and telephone centres.

Remember to check the difference between GMT and the time in the country where you are spending the winter. Calls at 2 a.m. are not appreciated!

EMAIL

This is the simplest, cheapest and most reliable way to keep in touch. Anyone can set up an email address for use on computers abroad. Hotmail and Yahoo are two companies which offer the service free. You can make sure in advance that there are internet cafés in your chosen resort, by logging on to www.cybercafes.com or www.netcafeguide.com/

countries.html or searching the net for 'internet cafés (plus location)'. You should be able to find their names and addresses.

DAILY ROUTINE

Living abroad is quite different from being on holiday. Holidays are a wonderful break from routine, an opportunity to sleep late in the mornings, spend self-indulgent hours on the beach or in the bar, dine lavishly each evening and dance the night away. After fifty weeks of duty well done, holidays are a chance to kick over the traces. Needless to say, such a life would be disastrous in the longer term! We all need routine. It provides a comfortable, secure framework for our lives. Without it, we have too many choices to make, we feel adrift and vaguely dissatisfied.

The routine need not be arduous. Something as simple as tuning in early each morning to the news on the BBC World Service, taking a walk after breakfast, buying a newspaper from the same stand and spending half an hour over coffee or tea in the same café are enough to give shape to the morning and, just as important, to give a sense of belonging. You will pass the time of day with the newsvendor and you will become known and be welcomed in the café. You will begin to feel less of an outsider.

FOOD AND DRINK

Meals are an important part of the routine. If you are not on a full-board package, it makes financial sense to have a picnic lunch (either in your hotel room or out of doors, depending on the weather) and to take your main meal of the day in a restaurant.

Supermarkets are tempting, because it is so much simpler to go round alone with a trolley and have no necessity to speak to anyone in a foreign language. But shopping for your picnic can be another important way of establishing yourself in the community. Once you have made the initial effort with the local baker, grocer and fruiterer, you will get a friendly greeting whenever you appear in the shop. And if you find it impossible to learn the words for what you want, pointing is understood in any language! You can signal to them that you need to have the price written down, so that you can see what you have to pay.

For the main meal of the day, there will no doubt be a number of restaurants where you will become a regular. You will have the leisure to inspect them all and note the ones where the locals eat, as they are always the best value for money. Although it is extremely agreeable to push the boat out once or twice a week and go to a really smart restaurant with crisp white linen, a battery of cutlery and an extensive wine-list, there will be many typically local places, where the food will be just as good, if not better, for a fraction of the cost. They are not usually called restaurants: in Greece and Turkey, for example, they are *taverna* and *lokanta* and in Italy *trattorie*. They are often places without a menu, where the visitor peers into the pans and points to the dishes he fancies. Few tourists eat there and those who do are greeted with warmth and even pride that foreigners have bestowed the honour of their patronage on a modest establishment. And, of course, if you pine for the occasional pizza, few resorts in the world are without their American-style fast food outlets.

On food generally, whether in the shops or the restaurants, it saves considerable expense to choose the local products – as well as adding to the interest of your stay. Imported brie or roquefort cheese will obviously be very expensive, and may be no more delicious than any one of the array of home-produced cheeses on the counter. Imported English jams, Cadbury's chocolates, Mars Bars and Kellogg's cornflakes are all available – at a price. But why not try the local alternatives? You may even come to like them better. And do try the local wines, beers and spirits as alternatives to Heineken and expensive imported Scotch whisky.

In restaurants, if the most commonly served meat is the local lamb, it will be cooked in a variety of interesting ways. An imported steak, on the other hand, will be expensive and may well turn out to be a tough, over-cooked disappointment when it arrives. It is much safer, as well as cheaper, to stick to the local produce, in whose preparation the local chefs will be masters.

In cafés, it pays to get used to the local beverage, whether it be small glasses of black tea, Turkish coffee, mint tea, or tea boiled up with the milk and sugar, Indian style. The alternatives are expensive and often disgusting; and they can be unsafe, if they contain unboiled, unpasteurized milk. So try to go native when you are out, and make your own tea and coffee as you like them in your hotel room.

CHORES
Life abroad is stress-free and easy, because there are no obligations and no round of domestic chores. But a few small, humdrum occupations can be very soothing and can help to keep a grip on reality. For instance, although hotel laundry services are often very cheap and quick, I find that I actually enjoy washing my own blouses and underwear. It makes a nice change from all that leisure!

MAKING FRIENDS
Even in a tropical paradise, 'no man is an island' and we all need friends. The lucky few may have one or two introductions as a beginning, but most people have to start from scratch. Even those on a long-stay package organized by a British firm will at first find themselves in a rather daunting sea of similarly friendless strangers and will have to make the effort to establish a social circle. The key to success is to let go of British reserve, to be open and receptive to the well-meant approaches of others and to be prepared to take the initiative, when necessary. Shrinking violets will shrink into their own loneliness. If there are English-speakers at the next table in the café, and you like the look of them, there is no reason on earth why you should not open up a conversation with them. And if that goes well, you

may like to invite them over to your table for another coffee, or invite them to meet you for a drink in the evening. I once jumped up to interpret for an American couple, who were having difficulty in ordering their cakes in French in a tea-shop in Chamonix. Forty years and a number of visits later, we are still firm friends.

Language may be a barrier to relations with the local people, but if they have any English, they are usually eager to practise it. You will soon learn to recognize the bores, the con men and the agents of the local carpet-sellers. The rest, with a little friendliness on your part, will be pleased to put their local knowledge at your disposal and may well provide your entrée to the local community. When you are invited to a meal with a local family, you will know that you have really arrived.

CLUBS AND PASTIMES

Opportunities for getting to know people in a casual way are there all the time, in the hotel and out of it, and should never be neglected. But a surer way to make friends is through shared interests. The bowls enthusiast, the tennis player, the windsurfer and the horseman will soon track down the appropriate facilities for the pursuit of their sports. Many of these activities have their own clubs, which is a great social advantage. A walk through the marina will soon bring yachtsmen into contact with their fellow Britons, who are either in the charter business or are living a life of ease on board their boats in warmer climes.

Keen golfers need to do careful research in advance. Most of the national tourist offices in London provide booklets listing the courses in their country, with full details of their designers, the number of holes, the handicap required and the availability of golf clubs for hire. They also give the green fees and the cost of temporary membership of the golf clubs. Costs vary considerably and may well influence your final choice of destination. A golfing package through a travel agent, which includes free club membership, green fees and hire of carts or buggies as well as clubs, may turn out to be the best buy.

Bridge clubs may be harder to find, but if you take the initiative and pin a notice on the hotel board, or put a card in the supermarket window, you may soon be the centre of a flourishing circle. If you say in the notice that you can speak a little French, Spanish or whatever, that will serve as an indication that you are willing to play bridge with the locals, or with tourists of other nationalities. The rules of the game are international and, provided you all know them, there will be no necessity for fluency in other languages. You just need to establish the words for the suits. The same approach can be used for chess, backgammon, or whatever game you enjoy.

Hotels catering for package holidaymakers usually offer whist drives, bingo and dancing in the evenings. Those who are not on a winter package will find it worthwhile to visit the hotels of those who are, as the representatives may be very happy for you to join in the activities of your choice.

In fact, enthusiasts will always find companions, if they keep their eyes and ears open and are prepared to make the first move. If you are a reasonable backgammon or mahjong player, why not challenge one of the locals, when you see the board temptingly placed outside a Turkish teahouse or a Malaysian shop? Your opponent will be delighted to have a game and language will be no barrier, as you will both know the rules.

But what are the possibilities for the non-sporting, who do not play indoor games?

VOLUNTARY WORK

If there is an English church, a synagogue or a church offering occasional matins or mass in English, it is a good idea to go along and make yourself known. Attendance at these local churches will provide an opportunity to meet some of the permanent British residents and perhaps be of assistance to them. Churches generally run a voluntary service programme, as well as social events, such as whist drives, and they are always trying to raise money. Extra help in visiting the old and lonely (now quite a problem in some parts of Spain, where people who sold up in England and bought villas at the age of sixty now find themselves sick and alone at eighty), shopping for the housebound, helping to escort school parties and selling bric-à-brac at the jumble sale will all be welcome. And if you have special skills, such as first aid training, the church may well be able to put you in touch with the local Red Cross and ease your entry on to their rota. Some churches overseas even have a team of volunteer prison visitors, who are prepared to travel to the major gaols to cheer up British prisoners. If you remain alert and open to possibilities, you will eventually find a very satisfying niche. There is nothing like feeling useful to give a spring to the step.

CULTURAL ACTIVITIES

Those spending the winter in or near a city will have a choice of exhibitions, concerts and plays to attend. They may even find that there is a branch of the British Council, which is a wonderful facility, as it offers a good library and a reading room with the previous day's British newspapers as well as a programme of British cultural events. Those who are not in a city will be less fortunate, but they should be sure to seize every opportunity that presents itself. A winter concert or an art exhibition, even if it is not to their taste, will be a good place to make contacts. On the whole, the smaller the resort, the fewer organized cultural events there are, but the easier it is for those with similar interests to find one another.

PROFESSIONAL CONTACTS

Teachers, doctors, nurses, architects, businessmen, lawyers and other professional people can easily establish contact with their local co-professionals, who will almost certainly be able to speak

English. Even without an introduction, it is possible to contact a local school, factory or clinic and arrange a visit. They will be delighted to meet you, show you round and exchange international views. You may even be invited to address a meeting or give some professional advice. Because of the employment legislation, it is simpler not to accept money for any of these services, unless they are on a major scale (see Chapter 5). The rewards are the social contact and the interest which will inevitably flow from the meeting.

LEARNING THE LANGUAGE

Some larger resorts run courses in the local language and the customs of the country especially for tourists. Do sign on for them, as they bring groups of visitors together with local teachers. And any improvement in facility with the language is a help. Offering your own services in return as a teacher of English is mentioned elsewhere, but it is worth repeating that this is a splendid way of making local friends. Conversation practice can take place in a café and can be informal and pleasurable for both parties.

SIGHTSEEING

It is obviously better to draw up a list of all the local historical sites, beauty spots, wild life parks and museums and spread the visits over the whole stay, rather than to rush round them all in the first fortnight. Organized coach tours are trouble-free, but they are quite expensive and quite unnecessary, if you have a whole winter at your disposal. Local buses and taxis are much more fun; and finding a remote archaeological site for yourself, after two changes of bus and a five-mile cross-country walk, gives a wonderful sense of achievement. You also have the site to yourself and can take as much time as you like to explore it.

Longer trips, of a weekend or even a week, can make very welcome breaks. Travel light, taking a few belongings in a backpack or small suitcase, and leave most of your luggage in your hotel. If you are lucky and hotel business is slack, you may even be able to leave all your possessions in your room, free of charge.

FLORA AND FAUNA

Those who are interested in wildlife should take all the appropriate reference books with them, as they are usually easier to obtain in Britain than they are abroad. In any case, books on birds and insects written in Thai or Turkish will be of limited use! Bird-watchers should be careful in most countries not to train their binoculars on bridges, harbours and factories, as the police are very sensitive about spying.

WORKING

THE PROFESSIONALS

The fortunate few, such as professional photographers and established writers, can pursue their careers just as well abroad as they can at home. And if they are self-employed and can demonstrate that their journey was solely and exclusively for work purposes, they may even be able to set their travel and hotel expenses against tax! Most will have a ready market for their work in Britain, but if they wish to sell their work locally, they must check up on local employment legislation and declare their earnings on their annual tax return (see Chapter 5). Those with technical, financial or managerial experience might consider applying to British Executive Services Overseas, 164 Vauxhall Bridge Road, London, SW1V 2RB (Tel: 020 7630 0624). This voluntary organization sends experienced, retired applicants abroad on special two- or three-month advisory projects and pays their travel expenses. An assignment of this length could be combined with a holiday in the country to produce a full winter in the sun. To my knowledge, this is the only organization taking volunteers for such a short tour abroad. Most voluntary agencies require a commitment of at least two years.

CASUAL WORK
See Chapters 3 and 5 for teaching English as a Foreign Language, which is virtually the only type of casual employment available.

NEWCOMERS TO SELF-EMPLOYMENT
If you have a hobby which you would like to turn into a trade, a winter abroad is your ideal opportunity to try your hand. If you have always wanted to write a novel or submit articles to newspapers, you will have months of freedom from telephone calls and small chores, when you can sit down every morning to write.

This is not the place for advice to would-be authors, but there is one word of caution. As far as articles are concerned, travel is a very competitive market, with most articles produced in-house. Even though your work may be very good, you may not be able to sell it to a national newspaper. A more hopeful approach might be one to your local newspaper. Get in touch with the editor before you leave home, submitting ideas for articles, and see if you can stimulate interest in advance. Articles on topical issues, as they relate to your chosen destination, may be more attractive than straightforward descriptive travel writing – an environmental slant, food and drink, education, the position of women are a few examples. The *Writers' and Artists' Yearbook*, published by A & C Black, gives helpful advice on setting out your work for submission to publishers; it also has comprehensive lists of newspapers, magazines, publishers and agents, and the types of work they handle. The *Writer's Handbook*, published by Macmillan, is also very useful.

Amateur photographers who are not already known for their work can use the winter to build up a really interesting portfolio. The *Freelance Photographer's Market Handbook*, published by BFP, is an invaluable guide to the types of photograph in demand. It lists potential publishers and photographic agencies by subject, as well as giving general advice on the presentation of work. Like bird-watchers, photographers need to be cautious. Be careful when you point your camera at bridges, prisons, refineries and other installations which might be important for national security, otherwise you might be accused of spying. In some countries, husbands may be averse to your taking photographs of their wives; in others it is believed that the camera robs the subjects of their souls. It is wise to ask permission in any country, and only polite, before photographing people. In less developed countries, a small payment is much appreciated.

Painting and drawing for the really talented are other obvious candidates for conversion to professional status, as is the carving of small items in local varieties of wood. Daily practice throughout the whole winter will do wonders for your technique and you will build up a good selection of work for exhibition on your return – or for sale to your fellow travellers.

Designing tapestry and knitwear in local patterns, or dresses based on local styles, may produce saleable ideas or finished items; and the collection of local recipes may be the basis of a cookery book or a series of articles. In fact any practical skill which does not require cumbersome equipment can be developed and enriched by the stimulus of your new cultural environment.

THE ENTREPRENEUR

Finally, a word to the businessman, the born entrepreneur. If you keep your eyes open, who knows what ingenious exportable item you may not spot on a local market stall. It could be the start of a new import–export business.

OBJECTIVES

Whatever your interests, life is much more rewarding if you are motivated by some long-term project, something which gives shape to your days and carries you along on its own momentum. It may be anything – improving your golf handicap, learning to ride a horse or a motorcycle, knitting a jersey for every member of the family (wool is always available, but take your own needles and patterns), collecting and pressing all the local wild flowers, making a set of tapestry covers for the dining-room chairs, learning the language, learning to play the recorder, raising money for the local hospital, writing a book . . . The list is endless and there is something for everyone. So give thought to your winter project and go prepared. Lazing by the swimming pool, even in perfect weather, is a short-lived pleasure.

BONUSES

Escaping the winter should be a pleasurable and interesting experience, beneficial to health and even to the pocket. But there are other, less tangible, rewards.

People in the South and East have different sets of values. They may not be punctual; their telephone system may be erratic; they may smile sweetly when you complain about the lavatory cistern, then do nothing to get it repaired. For those of us brought up in the West, where briskness and efficiency are highly regarded, these are maddening failings and it is very easy to get steamed up about them. But there is another side to the coin. When your friend finally arrives for his appointment, when the plumbers finally appear to mend the cistern, they will give you their undivided attention for as long as it takes. There will be no looking at watches, skimping the work, fidgeting to be off to the next appointment. You will benefit, to the detriment of the rest of their day's schedule, because they put their relations with people first. Time is less important.

One evening in Turkey I was rushing along the road to catch the last post when a Turk at a bus stop asked me, in English, 'Why are you so angry?' The question pulled me up sharply. I was not angry; I was just in a hurry to get to the post office. But *why* was it so urgent to get there that evening? Tomorrow morning's post would do just as well. Why not relax and smile, instead of haring along the road, looking like thunder?

If you are living in their country, it helps to look at things from their point of view. Sympathize with them if the telephone poses problems; it's not their fault. Smile if they are late for an appointment; after all, you too have all the time in the world. Read the local English-language newspaper, if there is one, to learn their economic and political preoccupations. Take an interest in the fortunes of the local football teams. Be much readier to chat with those you meet daily. They will appreciate it so much and you will have learned a valuable lesson – patience. You will find that your tolerance and open-mindedness grow markedly as the winter advances.

The other major change may well be your attitude towards possessions. You will have to manage throughout a whole winter on the contents of your suitcase; you will live in a hotel room, which will be functional, but sparsely furnished; and you will probably learn to get around without a car. At first, you will miss the refinements of your own home. But if my own experience is anything to go by, you will gradually come to terms with this simpler way of life and even begin to enjoy your freedom from possessions – all those items which have to be paid for, maintained, cleaned and insured. They eat up money and time, and they're only things! I still miss a few home comforts when I am abroad, such as my own blend of freshly-ground coffee in the mornings, but they are small items. I have learned to be content with little – and when our planet is fast running short of resources, that may be no bad thing.

GOING HOME

Unlike those who have sold up and moved abroad, you will have your own home and the green of the English summer to look forward to. You may need to buy an extra suitcase for the winter's accumulations and the local specialities you are taking home as gifts. But don't forget the locals. Do leave behind in your room, or give to the local church, any clothing or other items you can spare. In many countries they still turn collars and cuffs and your cast-off shirts may be someone else's treasure.

PART II WHERE TO GO

INTRODUCTION

INDEX OF COUNTRIES

CRITERIA FOR INCLUSION IN THE LIST

Warm winter climate
Good communications with home
Good internal communications for touring
Pleasant lifestyle
Political stability
Value for money

The list includes all the popular destinations and a few relatively exotic ones. It is by no means a comprehensive list of all possible countries. Using the check-lists and strategies in Part I, the enterprising traveller could spend happy, successful winters in a number of other locations.

Arrangement of material   The information on each country is set out in a standard format. This enables direct comparisons to be made.

Starter hotels   These are comfortable hotels in central locations, offering private facilities unless otherwise stated. They are in the middle price bracket.

Hotel prices   The travel market has been desperate for custom since September 11 and there has never been a better time to strike a bargain. Many hotels have simply stopped printing their rates, or even giving them over the phone, because in fact, in many resorts, any reasonable offer will be accepted. This has made it extremely difficult to quote realistic rates for the Starter Hotels.   Just treat them as starting points for haggling and be bold!

All prices quoted here are for a double room (i.e. for both people, not per person) for one night, as this is the way prices are normally quoted abroad.   Take care when comparing these prices with those of package holidays, as tour operators always give prices per person, based on two sharing.

THE FACT FILE

The following information has been found to apply to virtually every country in Part II:

Tipping   is generally 10 to 15 per cent of the bill.

Telephone   International direct dialling is possible from every country. Phonecards are available and most operators speak English.

email   Cybercafés abound and many hotels have internet and email facilities for their guests.

Television and radio   Satellite television is available in large hotels everywhere and the BBC World Service is obtainable on any short-wave radio (frequencies to be found in the magazine *BBC on Air* – see Chapter 10).

Newspapers   *Time*, *Newsweek* and the *International Herald Tribune* are available everywhere. British newspapers can be found on newspaper stalls in most major cities.

Inoculations against tetanus and polio are advisable for every country; only the additional requirements are given.

The odd exception to the above appears in each country's Fact File, generally under *Miscellaneous*.

Guidebooks   All the countries listed are well covered and your choice of guidebook will depend on your taste and on the kind of information you require. For straightforward facts – the nuts and bolts of travelling, such as reliable hotels and restaurants, bus services, where to catch trains – the Lonely Planet and Rough Guide series are hard to beat.

Websites   Most of the countries have official tourist sites, which are easy to track down on the internet.

The facts contained in this section have been checked very carefully. But regulations change, prices change and hotels change management. Please check vital information, such as the requirements for visas or work permits, before you leave home; and please inform us of any errors, or any changes in the standard of the hotels recommended.

THE MEDITERRANEAN

CYPRUS
Cyprus, where Aphrodite the Greek goddess of love and beauty, was born of the sea-foam, is the third largest island in the Mediterranean. Sheltered by the land masses of Turkey and the Middle East, it is the second warmest (after Tunisian Djerba). Where it comes first and reigns supreme is in its attraction to the British as a winter holiday island.

Cyprus enjoys on average 340 days of sunshine a year, with a few cool, rainy days in December and January. Two mountain ranges, a fertile central plain, forests, cliffs and sandy beaches provide an infinite variety of scenery, vegetation and wildlife, while the monuments of this much-coveted island could fill a lifetime of study and exploration.

Unfortunately, conflict between the Greeks and Turks has split the island in two, but this has not detracted from the friendliness of the Cypriots and the welcome they offer to visitors in both halves. They even speak English and drive on the left-hand side of the road!

Climate
Maximum and Minimum Coastal Temperatures

Oct	Nov	Dec	Jan	Feb	Mar	Apr
27	23	18	16	17	19	22
17	14	11	9	9	10	12

High Season   April to October

THE REPUBLIC OF CYPRUS (GREEK)
This constitutes two-thirds of the island and is the main tourist area.

Travelling there Direct flights to Larnaka and Paphos from a number of UK airports. Ferries from Athens to Limassol and Larnaka.

Travelling around Excellent bus services (none on Sundays); shared taxi services. Car, motorcycle and bicycle hire.

Travelling abroad Ferries to Athens (Piraeus), Israel (Haifa) and Egypt (Port Said). Limited winter ferry services to other Mediterranean islands.

Travelling to Northern Cyprus It is possible to get a day pass. Cars must be left in the car park of the Ledra Palace, Nicosia, near to the one crossing-point.

Where to stay For winter living, avoid the new towns, such as Agia Napa, which have grown up in response to tourist demand. They are virtual ghost towns out of season. Choose instead a genuine Cypriot town, which continues to buzz with activity long after the summer tourists have folded their beach umbrellas and gone home.

Paphos, for 800 years the capital of the island, would be my first choice. It combines the fascination of its glorious past with the good hotels and restaurants expected of a tourist destination. If you can cope with the gentle climb, the Upper City (Ktima Paphos) around Gladstone Street is more interesting in winter than the beaches of the Lower City (Kato Paphos). The bay is warm and sheltered, with impressive mountains behind; the harbour's tavernas, fish restaurants and cafés are ideal places to spend a lazy morning; and the temple and baths of Aphrodite, the Roman houses with their spectacular mosaics, the Byzantine churches and the pillar where St Paul was scourged all provide ample occupation.

Larnaka lies in a sheltered bay on the east coast. Built on the site of Mycenaean Kition, it is a prosperous Cypriot town with a palm-lined promenade and the smartest shops on the island. Commercial development has not ruined it. There are still cobbled streets and historical treasures to explore. The nearby salt lakes are the winter home to flamingos, wildfowl and swans, making Larnaka an attractive choice for natural-ists.

Nicosia, the capital, would be a sad place to stay, though it is rich in museums; the UN Green Line and the damaged buildings would be constant reminders of Cyprus' unhappy division.

Limassol is too industrialized. The mountain resorts of the Troodos are fine for a weekend's skiing or a spring ramble in good weather (see *Landscapes of Cyprus*, Sunflower Books, for suggested walks), but are too chilly for an entire winter.

Accommodation Hotels are classified by the Cyprus Tourist Organization and cover the whole range of price and comfort. Tour operators have long-stay packages in the most popular resorts and those wishing to spend the winter in a three- or four-star hotel are advised to book through a UK company. Depending on the firm, resort and hotel, prices start at about £115 a week per person, half board, including flights and transfers; from about £65 a week per person self-catering. Some firms include a few days' car hire. Independent travellers will be pleased to know that Cyprus has not yet been swallowed whole by the big travel firms. There are still small hotels and pensions, where it is possible to winter economically, and palatial five-stars for those with the means. Most actually print their off-season discounts (usually 24 to 40 per cent) and are prepared to go lower for a longer stay.

Starter hotels

Hotel New Olympus, Vronos 12, Paphos. This quiet hotel has sea views, gardens and a pool.   CY£43 (£46).

Sandbeach Castle, Piyale Pasha, Larnaka. A well-managed small hotel on the shore.   CY£43 (£46).

Double rooms in pensions and small hotels in and around both resorts can be found for £6 or £7 a night, before discounts.

Nightlife   Bouzouki music and dancing in the tavernas. Evening entertainments in the tourist hotels. English pubs.

Food   The gastronomic delight of Cyprus is the *meze* (mixture), bits and pieces of everything on offer that day in the taverna, from salads and dips, through shellfish, kebabs, grilled meats and chicken to sweets. Sometimes as many as thirty tiny dishes follow one another in a slow procession, accompanied by warm pitta bread and good local wines. All the usual Greek and Continental fare. A wide variety of fresh vegetables and fruit. Try the swordfish and *koulouri*, a local sesame seed bread. The national drink is *ouzo*, an aniseed-flavoured grape spirit.

Tourists and expatriates A third of all tourists to Cyprus are British and there are British military bases at Akrotiri and Dhekelia. The island's British past makes it an attractive retirement destination: over 3,000 Britons are permanent residents, while many more own property.

Leisure activities Greeks, Egyptians, Phoenicians, Assyrians, Byzantines, Richard Coeur de Lion, the Knights Templar, the Venetians and the Turks all held the island until 1878, when it came under British rule. This chequered past has resulted in a wealth of monuments and museum artefacts. Cyprus is a bird-watcher's paradise, as it lies on one of the main migratory routes; the rare moufflon is protected in the Paphos forests; and spring is a riot of wild flowers, with many unique species. Watersports, parascending, sub-aqua diving, bowling and cycling. Golf has been strangely neglected, but the first course is now open just outside Paphos. Clubs for chess, bridge, photography, philately, ornithology, tennis, squash and shooting. Cinemas, theatres, concerts, courses in Byzantine music and art – everything imaginable is available.

FACT FILE

Money The currency is the Cyprus pound (CY£), divided into 100 cents. Sterling and traveller's cheques are easily exchanged; credit and charge cards accepted. ATMs in towns.

Travel documents A full UK ten-year passport gives entitlement to a three-month stay. Extensions on application to the Aliens' Office in any large town. NB You may be refused entry to the (Greek) Republic of Cyprus if your passport contains a North

Cyprus stamp. The difficulty can be overcome by asking North Cyprus immigration officials to stamp a piece of paper instead.

Importation of motor vehicles A costly process, as they must be brought by car ferry from Athens.

Circulation of traffic Left-hand side of the road. International road signs. Most notices are in English as well as Greek.

Electricity supply 240v AC. 13 amp square-pin plugs, as in England.

Television and radio A BBC World Service television channel. Radio One is a private English-language station. Programme Two of the CYBC has English news bulletins and many English programmes.

Newspapers and books Cyprus News, Cyprus Times, Cyprus Weekly. English bookshops. The British Council and the American Center in Nicosia have good libraries and newspaper reading rooms.

Time difference GMT +2 hours.

Drinking water Tap water is safe. Mineral water available.

Inoculations None required.

Medical assistance Most doctors and dentists speak English. Emergency medical treatment free to tourists.

Language Greek. Almost everyone speaks English.

Politics Cyprus was granted independence from Britain in 1960. There was a Greek president (Archbishop Makarios) and a Turkish vice-president (Fasal Kükük) to safeguard the interests of the two communities. After a turbulent period of co-existence and a takeover attempt by the Greek Colonels in 1974, Turkey invaded the north of the island. Since 1983 there has been a separate Republic of Northern Cyprus, recognized only by Turkey. A UN peacekeeping force holds the Green Line, but all UN efforts to reach a political settlement have failed. The Republic of Cyprus (Greek) is a member of the British Commonwealth.

Religion Greek Orthodox, with Armenian, Maronite, Coptic and Evangelical minorities. Anglican and Roman Catholic

Churches in Nicosia. Nicosia has a mosque, but no synagogue.
Shopping bargains   Lefkaritika lace, silver filigree, beaten copper, baskets, pottery. Leather shoes, bags and jackets. Spectacles and contact lenses.
Film   Print and slide film available, but at roughly twice UK prices. Take a supply.
Useful addresses

   Cyprus Tourism Organisation, 17 Hanover Street, WI
   020 7259 5959.
   Tourist Offices in all Cypriot Resorts. Excellent maps,
   literature and handbooks.
   High Commission of the Republic of Cyprus, 93 Park
   Street, London W1K 4ET, Tel: 020 7499 8272.
   British High Commission, Alexander Pallis Street, Nicosia,
   Tel: (2) 2–861125.
   British Council, 3 Museum Street, Nicosia.

THE TURKISH REPUBLIC OF NORTHERN CYPRUS

Northern Cyprus occupies about one-third of the island, including the Kyrenia mountain range and the wonderful sandy sweep of Famagusta Bay. It is a country waiting to be discovered. Although it shares the climate and natural beauty of Greek Cyprus, international aid has not been forthcoming and there has been little tourist development since 1983. Turkish hospitality, delicious Turkish food and the lack of high-rise tourist ghettos make it a very attractive option for independent travellers seeking a peaceful winter in unspoilt surroundings.
Travelling there   Direct flights from Heathrow by Cyprus Turkish Airlines. All other flights via Turkey. Ferries from Mersin and Silifke (S. Turkey).
Travelling around   Excellent bus and minibus services. Cars, motorcycles and bicycles for hire.
Travelling abroad   Ferries to mainland Turkey.
Travelling to Greek Cyprus   Entry from Northern Cyprus is not allowed by the Greek Cypriot authorities.

Where to stay   Kyrenia (Turkish Girne) is a friendly, easy-going town, built around its ancient horseshoe-shaped harbour. Dominated by its ninth-century castle, it offers sandy beaches to the north and wooded mountains to the south, where Byzantine abbeys and Gothic churches cling dizzyingly to crags. Seafood restaurants, pubs and outdoor cafés line the harbour front. The castle houses the world's oldest shipwreck – a vessel with all its cargo, which sank in a storm off Girne around 3,000 BC.

Famagusta (Turkish Gazimagusa or Magusa), embraced by its perfect Venetian ramparts, was once one of the richest cities in the Mediterranean, with 365 churches, one for each day of the year. St Nicholas Cathedral, where the Lusignan Kings were crowned (1192–1489) is the finest Gothic building on the island; it now serves as a mosque. North of the city are the extensive ruins of Greek Salamis and wonderful sandy beaches.

Unfortunately, accommodation here is limited to a pair of over-expensive beach resorts, way out of town, and the more reasonably priced Hotel Sema on the Nicosia Road (£10). They would be useful for overnight stays, but not for long-term residence.

The mountain resorts are not recommended for a winter stay either, although they make excellent walking on fine days. Divided *Nicosia* (Turkish Lefkoşa) is a sad city, but well worth day trips or weekends to visit the museums, mosques and covered bazaar.

Accommodation   All hotels are classified by the Hotels Board of Northern Cyprus and conform to international standards of comfort and cleanliness. Most four- and five-star hotels are self-contained beach resorts outside the towns.

Starter hotel
Socrates Hotel, Kyrenia one block from the shore. A friendly, English-speaking hotel, with a swimming pool under the lemon trees. (£10).

Note: *Approximate prices are given in sterling because of the volatility of the Turkish lira.*

Discounts of at least 24 to 40 per cent should be available on long stays. Haggling is part of the Turkish way of life, so be bold!

Nightlife As in Turkey, dining out is the main evening activity. There are pubs, cafés and discos. Casinos in the major hotels.

Food It is worth visiting Turkish Cyprus for the food alone! In addition to the *meze* (see under Greek Cyprus), there are charcoal-grilled meats, fresh fish, interesting casseroles and vegetables, fruits and salads in season. The national drink is *raki*, an aniseed-flavoured grape spirit. Good local wines and beer.

Tourists and expatriates A few specialist firms, such as Voyages Jules Verne and Ramblers offer one-week packages, but most visitors are independent travellers. A few British residents.

Leisure activities There is a wealth of historical interest and a profusion of flora and fauna for the naturalist. Tennis courts and water sports facilities at the large hotels. But Northern Cyprus is not the place for those who need organized activities. It is a place to merge into the local life, to sit in the sun outside the cafés and make friends with the hospitable Turkish Cypriots. Skill at backgammon (tavla) is an asset.

FACT FILE

Please refer to the Greek Cyprus section, as many file entries are identical. Only the variations are listed below. See also the section on Turkey.

Money The currency is the Turkish lira (TL). Sterling, dollars and traveller's cheques are all encashable. Larger hotels and shops take credit cards. ATMs in the cities. Prices are agreeably low, but inflation is rampant, so change money in small quantities.

Travel documents A UK ten-year passport. No time limit. NB You may be refused entry to Greece or Greek Cyprus at a later date if your passport contains a Northern Cyprus stamp. Ask the Immigration Officer to stamp a piece of paper instead.

Importation of motor vehicles   More practicable than importation into Greek Cyprus, as cars may be driven across Turkey to Mersin or Silifke to catch the Kyrenia ferry.

Newspapers and books   *Turkish Daily News* and *Cyprus Today*. Blockbuster paperbacks in the large hotel bookshops. English bookshops in Kyrenia.

Medical assistance   Most doctors and dentists speak English. Treatment must be paid for.

Language   Turkish. English widely spoken.

Religion   Sunni Muslim, with small Greek Orthodox, Maronite and Armenian minorities. There is an Anglican Church in Kyrenia.

Miscellaneous   There is still National Service for three years in Turkey and it is the policy to send young recruits as far away from their homes as possible, to give them experience of life in another part of their large country. For farm boys from Central and Eastern Anatolia, it may well be the only time in their lives when they will travel beyond the next village. Northern Cyprus is a convenient place to deploy many of them and there may seem to be a daunting 'military presence' on the island – until you notice the young, homesick faces under the helmets.

Useful addresses

North Cyprus Tourist Office, 29 Bedford Square, London WC1. Tel: 020 7631 1930.

Tourist Offices in the main resorts.

Turkish Republic of Northern Cyprus, Office of the London Representative, 29 Bedford Square, London WC1. Tel: 020 7631 1920.

There is no British diplomatic representation in Northern Cyprus.

FRANCE

Sheltered from the cold north winds by *les Alpes Maritimes*, the Riviera is the only part of France to enjoy a reliably mild winter climate. In the great days of the train, when it provided Northern

Europeans with their most accessible sunshine, it was the fashionable place to be seen in winter. Elegant cities grew up to meet tourist demand and the rich and famous strolled along the promenades under the lemon and mimosa trees. But the charter flight has opened up more distant lands with warmer and more certain sun and the Côte d'Azur has now directed its energies to the summer trade. Winter is the unfashionable season, when the discerning few enjoy the warmth and beauty of this spectacular coast.

Climate

Maximum and Minimum Coastal Temperatures

Oct	Nov	Dec	Jan	Feb	Mar	Apr
20	16	14	12	13	14	16
16	12	10	8	8	10	12

Travelling there Flights to Nice. Train. Twice weekly Eurolines coach service. A pleasant drive.

Travelling around Excellent bus and train services. Car hire is quite expensive. Cycle hire.

Travelling abroad Italy is a short bus ride away.

Where to stay The warmest corner of the Riviera, favoured by Queen Victoria, whose statue graces the town, is *Menton*. Smaller than Nice or Cannes, it has a tranquil air, beautiful gardens, a pleasant promenade and a picturesque old town. Well served by public transport, it would be my first choice as a winter resort and a centre for sightseeing. For those who prefer a larger town, *Cannes* has always been popular with the British. It is smaller and friendlier than Nice, but still a sophisticated resort with elegant shops and wonderful fish restaurants down by the harbour.

Accommodation Many hotels close down for all or part of the winter, but those which are open are keen to get custom. Expect a reduction of at least 35 per cent on a long stay. In hotels with restaurants, full board is often an excellent bargain. Hotel prices in France are quite reasonable these days, compared with prices in England.

Starter hotels

Hotel Saint Michel, 1684 Promenade du Soleil, Menton (2 Star). A comfortable, small hotel on the seafront. €54 for a double room (£34).

Chalet de l'Isère, 42 Ave. de Grasse, Cannes (1-star). €46 for a double room (£30.50). An agreeable small hotel, interesting because it was the home of the writer Guy de Maupassant.

Nightlife Dining out, concerts, theatre. Casinos.

Food The food in restaurants is usually good value, though the wine is surprisingly expensive for a wine-producing country. French cuisine in general is too well known to need description, but the Riviera is noted for its fish, vegetables and fruit. Among the glories of France are its charcuteries, boulangeries, patisseries and fromageries. A bottle of wine and a selection from these mouth-watering shops will provide a picnic supper fit for the gods.

Tourists and expatriates The Riviera has always been popular with the British and there are residents scattered throughout the resorts. Menton has a particularly active community.

Leisure activities There is a spectacular coastline to enjoy, free of crowds, and the area is rich in modern art – Picasso in Antibes, Cocteau in Villefranche-sur-Mer and Menton, Matisse in Cimiez, Chagall in Nice and Renoir in Cagnes-sur-Mer – and Roman history, as the legions marched this way along the Via Julia Augusta into Spain. Botanists have the famous Hanbury Gardens, just over the border into Italy from Menton, and a profusion of spring flowers from January onwards. There are ten golf courses within easy reach. Swimming pools, tennis, boules, fishing. Menton has weekly concerts and a Wednesday lunch for English-speakers; Cannes has a wide range of cultural events. Nearby Monte Carlo has its world-famous Ballet and Opera. There is an English library attached to the Anglican Church in Menton, also bridge and whist clubs.

FACT FILE

Money   The currency is the Euro, divided into 100 centimes. No problems with sterling, traveller's cheques, or credit cards. ATMs widespread.

Travel documents   A ten-year British passport gives 90 days' residence. It is much easier to hop on a bus to Italy for the day and re-enter France than to go through the formalities for extensions.

Circulation of traffic   Right-hand side. International road signs.

Electricity supply   220v AC. Round two-pin plugs.

Television and radio   All in French.

Newspapers and books   No locally produced English-language newspapers. English books in Cannes; a few paperbacks elsewhere.

Time difference   GMT + 1 in winter.

Drinking water   Tap water is safe. France is the land of bottled water.

Inoculations   None required.

Medical assistance   Ask at your hotel or the tourist office for English-speaking practitioners.

Language   The French are as proud of their language as we are of ours and some knowledge of it is essential. English is spoken in some hotels and restaurants.

Politics   A bicameral parliamentary democracy with an executive president. France is a founder-member of the EC and one of the five permanent members of the UN Security Council.

Religion   Roman Catholic, with Islam now the largest minority religion. Holy Trinity Anglican Church, Rue Gal Ferrié, Cannes. Synagogue, Blvd. d'Alsace, Cannes. St John's Anglican Church, Ave. Carnot, Menton. Various Evangelical Protestant Churches.

Shopping bargains   None, except perhaps in the Winter Sales.

Film   All types and brands available at roughly UK prices.

Miscellaneous   Hotels and restaurants include a 15 per cent service charge in all bills, so that tipping is not expected. Most people simply leave the odd coppers for the waiter and round up the fare to the taxi-driver, no matter how great the distance. Tips are, however, expected in the really expensive restaurants. The French are still formal in their address, using Monsieur, Madame or Mademoiselle in their dealings with strangers. *S'il vous plaît* has superseded *garçon!* as the polite way to summon the waiter. Smart dressing and good grooming are still important, particularly in the evenings.

Useful addresses

French Government Tourist Office, 178 Piccadilly, London W1V 0AL, Tel: 020 7355 4747.

Excellent supply of literature both here and in local tourist offices.

French Consulate General, 21/23 Cromwell Road, London SW7 2DQ, Tel: 020 7838 2000.

British Embassy, 35 Rue du Faubourg St. Honoré, Paris 8ème, Tel: (1) 4451 3100.

British Consulates in Marseille and Nice.

GREECE

It is no accident that the tour operators omit Greece from their winter holiday brochures. The mainland is chilly and wet, while the islands are chilly, wet and windy. The one possible winter destination is Rhodes, which is sheltered to some extent from the worst of the weather by the Marmaris peninsula of Turkey. For those who wish to escape from tourists and merge into local life, Rhodes could be an interesting choice. But it is not for sun-worshippers.

Rhodes is the largest of the Dodecanese Islands. Its strategic situation at the very corner of the Turkish mainland, together with the fertility of its valleys, has ensured its commercial prosperity since the Bronze Age and endowed it with some of the world's finest military architecture. There is balmy winter sunshine on Rhodes, as is shown by the profusion of hibiscus and poinsettias, but the good spells are interspersed with rain, gale-force winds and even the occasional sprinkling of snow. Yet few destinations can provide the discriminating tourist with so many significant historical sites in so compact an area. There is ample indoor occupation for rainy days.

Climate

Maximum and Minimum Coastal Temperatures

Oct	Nov	Dec	Jan	Feb	Mar	Apr
24	20	17	15	15	16	20
18	15	12	10	10	11	13

High season   May to October.

Travelling there   Flights, usually via Athens. Regular ferry services throughout the year from Athens (Piraeus).

Travelling around   Excellent bus services, linking all the main sites and villages. Taxis are relatively inexpensive. Car, motorcycle and bicycle hire.

Travelling abroad   Ferries to Israel, Turkey (Marmaris), Cyprus and Italy (Brindisi), and to many Greek islands. A steep embarkation tax of around £32 is imposed on passengers leaving Rhodes for a foreign port.

Where to stay   The city of *Rhodes*, where the residents enjoy a sophisticated lifestyle. Elsewhere, there is so little winter tourism that most of the hotels and restaurants are closed.

Accommodation   Of the sixty or so three-star hotels in Rhodes City, few stay open in winter. In the Old City, within the fortifications, two very modest pensions with shared facilities offer double rooms at around €25 a night (£16).

Lindos has a few basic self-catering apartments, but as there is only one bar open and one restaurant, which cooks on occasional evenings, Lindos is a ghost town – wonderful for a day trip (take a picnic), but as a long-stay winter resort suitable only for hermits. From €25 a night for a double studio flat (£16). The buses pass through some charming villages, where there are rooms to rent. They might be worth exploring, if you wanted to learn Greek and become a part of local life.

Starter hotel

Hotel Hermes (3-star) in Rhodes new town. €42 for a double room (£28). A comfortable, well-heated hotel with an elegant coffee shop and views over Mandraki Harbour.

The few hotels and pensions which are open are prepared to offer 40 per cent off for a long stay. They are keen to get custom and hard bargaining might secure even greater reductions.

Nightlife   Smart cafés and cocktail bars, well patronized by the locals. Casino at the Grand Hotel.

Food   Rhodes is noted for its seafood – red mullet, tunny, langoustes, crabs, octopus and garfish – but in the winter, the seas may be too rough for fishing and the typical Greek tavernas are mostly shut. The locals have leapt into fast food with inexcusable zeal and the only offerings on winter evenings are pizzas, chicken and chips, hamburgers and toasted sandwiches. The Greek national drink is *ouzo*, a clear aniseed-flavoured grape spirit. Good beers and some Rhodian wine, though most is imported from the mainland.

Tourists and expatriates   A handful of British residents. Mandraki Harbour is a winter haven for British yachts. If you sit long enough in the sea-front cafés you will meet all the Britons on the island. Few winter tourists.

Leisure facilities   Greeks, Romans, the Knights of the Order of St John of Jerusalem, the Turks and finally the Italians all held the island at various stages and left their architectural and cultural marks. After a brief period under German occupation, Rhodes was returned to Greece in 1948. The walled Collachium, or citadel, where the Knights lived and built the Grand Master's Lodge, the great Hospital and the Auberges of the various Tongues, is possibly the finest ensemble of Gothic buildings anywhere in the world. At the other end of the island is Lindos, a Dorian acropolis standing high on a wild and craggy promontory, sheltering its tiny whitewashed port in the sandy bay beneath. Between Rhodes City and Lindos lie villages with Greek ruins, Byzantine churches of great beauty, medieval castles and monasteries. For walkers, there are the mountains and valleys with groves of orange, lemon, almond and olive trees, forests, terraced hillsides and windswept moors with aromatic shrubs. Golfers have the Afandou Club, half an hour from Rhodes on the Lindos bus. The Rhodes Sports Centre has tennis courts and there is a Riding Centre. Water sports in November and May. The locals are keen on backgammon.

FACT FILE

Money The currency is the Euro, divided into 100 cents. No problems with sterling, dollars, traveller's cheques, or credit cards. ATMs in towns.

Travel documents Three months' stay permitted on a full ten-year UK passport. Extensions on application to the local police.

Circulation of traffic Right-hand side. International road signs. Directions given in English as well as Greek.

Electricity supply 220v AC. Round two-pin plugs. Most of normal thickness, but a few sockets take the very fine variety.

Television and radio CBS News on Antenni Channel. English news on the radio at 7.30 a.m. (412 kHz).

Newspapers and books English-language *Athens News*. A limited selection of paperback novels in bookshops.

Time difference GMT + 2 hours.

Drinking water Tap water is safe. Plentiful mineral water.

Inoculations None.

Medical assistance Ask the hotel or tourist office for English-speaking doctors and dentists.

Language Greek, but English is widely spoken.

Politics Rhodes is a part of the Hellenic Republic, which is a member of the EC and NATO.

Religion Greek Orthodox. Easter and the Epiphany Blessing of the Sea are spectacular feasts. Protestant Church of St Francis in Meg. Konstandinou and Roman Catholic Santa Maria in Georgiou Papanikolaou. Synagogue in Perikleous in the Old Town. A number of mosques.

Shopping bargains   Rhodes is famous for its umbrellas! Jewellery, needlework, ceramics of Paradissi.

Film   Print and slide film available, but slightly more expensive than in the UK.

Useful addresses

Greek National Tourist Organization, 4 Conduit Street, London W1, Tel: 020 7734 5997.

Rhodes Tourist Office, corner of Makariou and Papagou, Tel: 23 255.

British Consulate, Rhodes City.

ITALY

Think of art, churches, sunshine, pasta, wine and *la dolce vita* and you have the popular impression of Italy. Despite the fact that its economy has lately outperformed those of its competitors, Italy manages to retain that aura of ease and joyful living which has been its main attraction since the days of the Grand Tour. The study of its art and architecture would fill a dozen lifetimes; and at the end of each day's exertions, there is always the welcoming table at the local trattoria. The down side is the winter climate. Italians from the peninsula actually winter in London to escape the freezing fog! Only two areas enjoy reliably warm, sunny weather: the Riviera and Sicily. But most hotels in Sicilian resorts close down in the winter, so the Riviera is the only sensible choice.

Climate
Maximum and Minimum Daily Temperatures
Riviera

Oct	Nov	Dec	Jan	Feb	Mar	Apr
20	16	14	12	13	14	16
16	12	10	8	8	10	12

High season   May to October

Travelling there   Scheduled flights to Nice and Genoa. Many budget flights, charters and discounted fares, so shop around.

Daily train services from London (Victoria). Eurolines coaches to the Riviera and Genoa.

Travelling around   Excellent train and bus services. For the motorist, the *autostrada* tolls are high, but the A roads, the *statali*, are free.

Travelling abroad   France is just along the coast.

Where to stay   The *Riviera dei Fiori* (Riviera of Flowers), like the neighbouring Côte d'Azur, is sheltered by the Alps from the cold north winds. Its popularity as a winter resort faded with the advent of charter flights to warmer, cheaper lands, but it is still an elegant strip of resorts along a spectacular coast. It becomes noticeably warmer and the mimosa, fuchsias and bougainvillea more luxuriant (even in January) as the road runs south-west towards the French border. *Bordighera* lies at the French end in the sheltered Bay of San Remo. It has enough vitality to keep up the interest out of season and it would be my own first choice, though others may have their own favourites which would serve equally well. For those who like city life, *Imperia*, the capital of the province, has much to commend it. Not a resort, though it has a fine sandy beach, it is a city where Italians live and work. Porto Maurizio, its harbour, has cobbled mediaeval streets and squares, and there are elegant shops at the modern end. If you want to be a resident rather than a tourist, Imperia is a typical Italian town, where immersion in local life would be a pleasure.

Accommodation   Hotel tariffs were deregulated in 1992 and immediately shot up by as much as 40 per cent. These price rises have made Italy one of the more expensive winter options. But prices do fall out of season and firm bargaining might produce a further reduction of 20 to 25 per cent on a long stay. The title of the establishment is not necessarily an indication of its price. *Hotel, albergo* or *pensione* seem to be used on the whim of the owner. *Locande, alloggi* and *affittacamere* are cheaper; the first two being simple rooms over a restaurant or café, while the third is furnished accommodation. Lists of addresses from local tourist offices.

Starter hotels

Hotel Bordighera and Terminus (3-star), Corso Italia 21, Bordighera. €52 for a double room (£35). A comfortable, centrally situated hotel with a garden.

Hotel Croce di Malta, via Scarincio, Porto Maurizio, Imperia (3-star). €54 for a double (£36). On the beach with a good restaurant.

Nightlife   On the Riviera, casinos, nightclubs, concerts, dining out.

Food   Italian cuisine is too well known to need a general description.

Tourists and expatriates   No great concentrations of British tourists. A few residents along the Riviera, mainly in the Bordighera/San Remo area. Out of season, some knowledge of Italian and a willingness to participate in local life are necessary.

Leisure activities   The Riviera offers relaxation – walks in the sun along the promenade, coffee on a terrace by the sea and perhaps a game of tennis or bowls. Bordighera has a flourishing Anglo-Ligurian Club and Golf Club. San Remo has concerts, museums and a casino, while the world-famous Monte Carlo Opera and Ballet is just up the coast. Within easy reach of the French Riviera and the Alps, the western end of the Riviera dei Fiori is a good centre for exploration. Botanists will be overwhelmed by the variety of flowers, trees and shrubs and by the famous Hanbury Gardens near Ventimiglia.

FACT FILE

Money   The currency is the Euro divided into 100 cents. Changing money at banks is very time-consuming, but ATMs are plentiful. Some retail outlets are still suspicious of credit cards.

Travel documents   A valid UK passport gives three months' residence. Extensions, on a full ten-year passport only, on application to the police. Those on the Riviera will find it simpler to take the bus into France and re-enter Italy.

Circulation of traffic   Right-hand side. International road signs. Note that motorways are signposted in green and other roads in blue – the opposite to most other countries.

Electricity supply   220v AC. Plugs usually have two round pins. In areas using three round pins, adaptors are available locally.

Television and radio   Infrequent news bulletins in English on Channel 2.

Newspapers and books   Popular paperbacks on sale in resorts.

Time difference   GMT + 1 hour in winter.

Drinking water   Tap water is safe. Plentiful mineral water.

Inoculations   None required.

Medical assistance   Ask at the hotel or tourist office for English-speaking doctors and dentists.

Language   Italian. English spoken in hotels and restaurants, but not in the countryside.

Politics   A parliamentary republic with a president and an electoral system which has produced over fifty unstable coalitions since 1946. The Italians, more than most people, flourish in spite of their politicians! A founder-member of the EC and a member of NATO.

Religion   Officially Roman Catholic, though there is a strong vein of anti-clericalism, particularly in the North. There is an Anglican Church in San Remo.

Shopping bargains   Leather coats, bags and gloves. Florentine paper goods. Watch the December and January sales for reductions in elegant clothing.

Film   All types and brands available, at roughly UK prices.

Useful addresses

Italian State Tourist Board, 1 Princes Street, London W1R 8AY, Tel: 020 7408 1254.

Tourist offices in most Italian cities and resorts.

Italian Consulate-General, 38 Eaton Place, London SW1X 8AN, Tel: 020 7235 9371.

British Embassy, Via XX Settembre 80a, Rome, Tel: (6)
4220 0001.
British Consulates: Via XII Ottobre 2, 13th Floor, Genova,
Tel: 010 564 833.

MALTA

Malta (17 by 9 miles) is the largest island in a small archipelago, which rises steeply from the Mediterranean, south of
Sicily. Its local name, Melitta, is derived from the Latin word
for honey (mel), one of the island's specialities; and honey is
the colour of its soft limestone rocks and buildings. Important
throughout history for its strategic situation, since World War
II the George Cross Island has turned its attention to tourism.
The energy and charm of the Maltese have worked wonders
on their crowded, treeless, riverless homeland. They have
exploited to the full its main tourist assets – its low rainfall,
pleasant year-round climate and its British past, making it a
warmer version of home to its half million or more British visitors. It is a relaxed, friendly and relatively inexpensive place
to spend a winter in the sun.

Climate

Maximum and Minimum Daily Temperatures

Oct	Nov	Dec	Jan	Feb	Mar	Apr
24	20	16	14	15	16	18
19	16	12	10	10	11	13

High season June to October

Travelling there Frequent scheduled and charter flights from a
number of British airports. Car ferries from Naples, Syracuse,
Catania and Reggio di Calabria.

Travelling around Excellent bus services on Malta and Gozo.
Regular ferries to Gozo. Occasional winter crossings to Comino.
Car hire is better value than taxis, though parking is a problem.
Bicycle and scooter hire.

Travelling abroad Regular ferries to Sicily and Southern Italy.
Occasional sailings to Southern Spain, Tunisia and Morocco.

Where to stay   Malta tilts down from the Dingli Cliffs on the south-west coast to the harbours and beaches of the north-east, where development is concentrated. As the island is small, all the resorts are within easy reach of the capital, Valletta, the centre of the transport system, so that location is a matter of choice rather than convenience. Malta is a rocky island and the less sprightly should be sure to choose a resort with a level promenade and shopping streets on a gentle slope, such as Sliema, rather than the rugged coastline of Bugibba and neighbouring northern resorts.

For those who like cities, *Valletta* is fascinating historically, with the lively modern Paceville nearby. Inland, away from the tourists, the old capital of *Mdina* and its neighbour, *Rabat*, have been backwaters since the Knights of the Order of St John of Jerusalem founded their new capital of Valletta in 1530, but they are elegant backwaters, with narrow cobbled streets and medieval palaces. Mdina is known as the Silent City or the Noble City, because most of Malta's aristocracy live there. Even quieter is the tiny, hilly island of *Gozo*, with its one small resort of Marsalforn and its rolling green farmland.

Accommodation   If you are looking for a three- or four-star hotel in Sliema, Bugibba, St Julian's, St Paul's Bay, Paradise Bay or T'axbiex (just outside Valletta), the main resorts, you cannot do better than book a long-stay package through a tour operator. Depending on the company and the class of accommodation, the price can be as low as £70 a week per person on half board, including flights and transfers; £25 a week per person self-catering. But those who prefer to be independent can still strike their own bargains, as hotel and self-catering tariffs fall by anything up to 40 per cent in winter and the skilful can negotiate even larger reductions on a long stay. There are plenty of budget-priced hotels and pensions, even in the popular resorts. Valletta is the best starting point, if you wish to inspect various locations before choosing.

Starter hotel

British Hotel (2-star), 267 St Ursula Street, Valletta. Well situated, with stunning views over the Grand Harbour. Garden, restaurant and bar. Lm 12–20 for a double with breakfast (£18–£30). Reductions for a long stay.

Nightlife   Paceville, a suburb of Valletta, is the place for the laser discos and all-night bars, especially at weekends. More sedate pleasures, from bridge to barn dances, in the tourist hotels. Casino at St Julian's.

Food   Maltese cuisine is influenced by Southern Italian, its soups, seafood and pasta differing little from the dishes on offer in Sicily. The preponderance of British tourists has ensured a good supply of meat and two veg. and sausage and mash. Local specialities are rabbit (*fenech*), cooked in wine and tomatoes, cheese pasties (*pastizzi*), spicy beef rolls (*bragioli*) and a macaroni, egg and cheese pie (*timpana*). The deliciously chewy bread is unique to Malta. Honey, a wide range of vegetables and fruit. Local wines from the terraced vineyards are very palatable.

Tourists and expatriates   The British predominate in both categories. A resident community of 1,000 is boosted by over 3,000 other property owners.

Leisure activities   For such a small island, Malta offers a wealth of historical interest. Phoenicians, Romans, Arabs, Normans, Spanish, French and British have all left their monuments and their influence, but no period in Malta's past is greater than that of the Knights of St John, who landed there in 1530 and built one of the world's finest and most impregnable military complexes at Valletta. The religious devotion of the Maltese, the patronage of the Knights and the influence of Spanish baroque have produced churches of amazing size and richness; Maltese church festivals, with processions, coloured lights and fireworks, are still the main events on the island's calendar. Diving, riding, cycling, bowls, walking. (see *Landscapes of Malta and Gozo*, Sunflower Books). The Marsa Sports club, just south of Valletta, offers golf (18 holes), tennis, squash, archery, swimming and horse-racing. Many of the large tourist hotels have indoor swimming pools and provide a range of entertainments. During the Manoel Theatre Season (October to May), there are concerts, operas and plays. International Choir Festival in October. Films, exhibitions and other cultural activities.

FACT FILE

Money   The currency is the Maltese lira (Lm or #), divided into 100 cents. No problems with foreign currency, traveller's cheques or credit cards. ATMs in most towns.

Travel documents   A full British ten-year passport allows three months' stay. As no extension is possible, it is necessary to go across to Sicily and re-enter for a further three months.

Circulation of traffic   Left-hand side. International road signs.

Electricity supply   240v AC. Flat three-pin plugs, as in Britain.

Television and radio   Daily English news bulletins. Some English and American programmes on both TV and radio.

Newspapers and books   The *Times of Malta* and the *Sunday Times* are the main English-language newspapers. *Where Malta* (monthly) gives bus routes as well as a calendar of events. Several good bookshops.

Time difference   GMT + 1 hour in winter.

Drinking water   Tap water is not recommended. Plentiful bottled water.

Inoculations   None required.

Medical assistance   English-speaking doctors and dentists. Citizens of the UK are entitled to free health care, under reciprocal arrangements.

Language   Maltese (thought to be a Semitic language, strongly influenced by Arabic and the Romance languages). English widely spoken, except in small inland villages.

Politics   A republic within the British Commonwealth. A president, unicameral parliament and an executive prime minister.

Religion   Devoutly Roman Catholic. Mass in English at too many resorts to list. St Paul's Anglican Pro-cathedral, Valletta, and Holy Trinity, Sliema. Church of Scotland, Methodist churches and synagogues. Details from the local tourist office.

Shopping bargains   Jeans, shoes, lace and handknits. Gozo is less expensive, though perhaps less sophisticated.

Film   All brands and types readily available, at roughly UK prices.

Miscellaneous   Despite tourism, the Maltese remain a devout and conservative people. No shorts or naked torsos in the churches.

Useful addresses

Malta Tourist Office, Unit C, Park House, 14 Northfields, London SW18 IDD. Tel: 020 8877 6990.

Malta High Commission, 36/38 Piccadilly, London, W1J OLE. Tel: 020 7292 4800.

British High Commission, 7 St Anne Street, Floriana, Malta, Tel: 233134/7.

British Council, 89 Archbishop Street, Valletta.

National Tourist Office, 280 Republic Street, Valletta.

Anglo-Maltese League Club, Merchants' Street, Valletta.

MOROCCO

Warmed by the Sahara to the south and cooled by breezes from the Atlantic and Mediterranean, Morocco has the perfect winter climate. It is a bridge between Africa, Islam and the West, an easy-going land where miniskirts and yashmaks are equally at home in its sophisticated cities. Inland lie the architectural gems of the former capitals of Fes and Marrakesh, still medieval in feel, and the Berber strongholds of the High Atlas and the oases. Like the British in India, the French during their protectorate built a modern city alongside each of the ancient walled medinas. This gives travellers a choice: they can either live in the West, in a three- or four-star hotel along a gracious jacaranda-lined boulevard, or they can go Moroccan in one of the more basic hotels within the ancient walls. Morocco has golden beaches, deserts and four magnificent mountain ranges. Because there is a touch of the exotic, the country has not yet been swallowed whole by the major tour operators. It is a fascinating and inexpensive land for the winter traveller to explore.

Climate

Maximum and Minimum Temperatures in Marrakesh and the South

Oct	Nov	Dec	Jan	Feb	Mar	Apr
28	23	19	18	20	23	26
14	9	6	4	6	9	11

Coastal resorts are less chilly at night than desert Marrakesh. Tangier and the north are about 5°C cooler than the south.

High season   Spring in the north; winter in the south.

Travelling there   Flights from the UK to all major cities. A cut-price ticket to Gibraltar or Malaga, followed by the bus to Algeciras, may save considerable money. Overland by train, coach or car to Algeciras or Gibraltar for the frequent car ferries to Tangier.

Travelling around   Fares are low on the excellent rail and road network. For longer coach journeys, it is worth paying the extra 10 to 15 per cent for the Pullmans run by the national CTM (Compagnie des Transports Marocains). There are large shared taxis and *petits taxis* for individuals. Inexpensive, but agree the price first. Car hire is not cheap, but bargain for a discount for longer periods. Cycle hire.

Travelling abroad   Spain. West Africa can be entered only from Algeria, as the Western Sahara south of Dakhla is out of bounds to tourists.

Where to stay   There are many wild and wonderful places to visit in Morocco, but most people like a comfortable base. My four suggestions are all very different from one another.

   Tangier's past as an international zone has given it a glamorous reputation. Once one of the most fashionable resorts in the Mediterranean, it was a haven for exiles and spies as well as for artists, writers and royalty. Although it is slightly seedier these days, it is well policed and probably less dangerous than many cities in the West. Cooler and rainier in the winter than the cities of the south, its kasbah, squares and smart cafés provide shelter and interest when the weather is unsuitable for the beach. There is a sizeable British resident community, a few British-run restaurants, and an Anglican Church.

Marrakesh, Churchill's winter favourite, is wonderfully situated beneath snow-capped mountains. No longer one of the major artistic and cultural centres of the Islamic world, it is taking advantage of its near-perfect winter climate to pull in the higher class tourist. Now is the time to stay there, before the package takeover is complete. The souks of the old city, with their quarters for spices, metalwork and inlaid wood, crowd around the Djemaa el Fna, the main square, which comes alive at sunset with fire-eaters, snake charmers, jugglers and performing monkeys. The new town has been carefully developed in a uniform terracotta colour, with wide boulevards of flowering trees and smart hotels with their swimming pools.

Agadir was devastated by an earthquake in 1960 and has been rebuilt as the perfect seaside resort. It is the main destination of the package tour operators and its superb winter climate makes it particularly attractive to the older, long-stay visitor, usually from France or Germany. It is possible to live here on full board, in an excellent hotel with its own beach and leisure facilities, and have nothing at all to do with Morocco. Yet there *is* another Agadir, separated from the immaculate pre-stressed concrete by parks and empty building-sites. Here the Moroccans live; here are some of the best restaurants in town; and here the two- and three-star hotels are pleased to welcome the independent traveller. Agadir is important as the starting-point for treks into the High Atlas, the Anti Atlas and the oasis towns of the Sahara. Its golden beaches, cleaned daily, offer every kind of water sport and it is warm enough all the year round to bathe in the Atlantic and dine out under the stars. There is an Alliance Franco-

Marocaine, which has a lively cultural programme of plays, films and lectures.

For those who like a smaller town, there are a number of sixteenth-century fortified Portuguese cities down the Atlantic coast. *El-Jadida* (Portuguese Mazagan) has ramparts enclosing a remarkable underground rain-water cistern (where Orson Welles filmed a scene from *Othello*) and the old houses of the medina. Beside it, the French built their 'Moroccan Deauville' with its elegant palm-shaded promenade along a perfect beach. El-Jadida is now a favourite holiday resort for the rich of Casablanca, who own villas there. A charming laid-back little town, very French in feel, with good communications. *Essaouira*, between El-Jadida and Agadir, is a similar resort, but slightly larger.

Accommodation   Moroccan hotels are Government-inspected and have official star-ratings. The five-stars may fix their own rates, but all other categories have official maxima and must display their prices at reception. Except for a few flophouses in the medinas, which are too basic for official recognition, Moroccan hotels are clean and well managed. Haggling is a way of life and reductions are always possible – up to 50 per cent in cooler Tangier; 20 to 25 per cent in the south. The exception is Agadir, where those requiring three- or four-star accommodation are advised to book an extended package.

Starter hotels

Tangier. For the bold, who are not afraid to stay just inside the walls of the medina, the crumbling glories of the old Continental (1-star A), once patronized by kings and potentates, is the only choice. This eccentric palace, Classical French above and Arabian Nights below, makes up for its shortage of private lavatories by its unique atmosphere and its terrace overlooking the port. 350 dhs, for a double room (£23).

In the new city, the Rembrandt (3-star A). A gracious, spacious hotel, keen to please the independent traveller.

Swimming pool, restaurant, salon de thé. 800 dhs. for a double (£53).

Marrakesh. Hotel de la Menara (3-star A). A modern hotel, furnished in Moroccan style, in a quiet side street near the ramparts of the old city and the central Place de la Liberté. Gardens and swimming pool. Restaurant disappointing, but plenty of alternatives nearby. 350 dhs. for a double (£23).

Agadir. Hotel Sindibad (2-star A). A charming hotel, overlooking a small square filled with magnolias, hibiscus, lavender and roses. Roof terrace with small swimming pool, restaurant, salon de thé and ice cream parlour. 285 dhs. for a double (£19).

El-Jadida. Hotel de Provence (2-Star A). Appointed like a French provincial hotel, it has the best restaurant in town. Its genial, well-informed English owner has recently died, but his partner has promised to maintain standards. 270 dhs. for a double room (£18).

Nightlife Everything from discos to belly-dancing in the larger towns. Cafés and restaurants elsewhere.

Food Moroccan food is delicious. If they advertise *cuisine française*, it really *is* French, as are their bread, croissants and brioches. The local cuisine combines sweet and savoury. *Tajines* are stews of any meat or fish, cooked slowly in an earthenware pot, packed with fresh vegetables and a few prunes, raisins or almonds. Try *harira* a spicy soup with a lentil base; *bstilla*, a filo pastry pie of ground pigeon and almonds, dusted with icing sugar; and *couscous*, steamed grain semolina with a sauce of meat and/or vegetables. The fish markets are a revelation; fruit and vegetables are excellent and cheap.

As Moroccans are Muslim, they are not supposed to drink alcohol, but it is available in all tourist hotels and restaurants – at a price. Smaller local restaurants are unlicensed, but are sometimes prepared to let clients bring in their own wine, discreetly. Ask first. They whisk it away into the kitchen and it reappears in Coca-Cola or lemon Fanta bottles, depending on its colour. Mint tea is the national beverage.

Tourists and expatriates   Tangier has a resident Anglo-American community. Agadir and Marrakesh are attracting British winter holidaymakers in increasing numbers, though the overseas residents are mostly French.

Leisure activities   Phoenicians, Romans, Arabs, Portuguese and French have all left their monuments and traditions in Morocco, often conquering the native Berbers, but never suppressing their culture. Those with an interest in history will merely scratch the surface in the course of a winter. Unfortunately, Morocco is the only Islamic country other than Saudi Arabia to bar the infidel from their mosques, so that many of the wonders of Moorish architecture are inaccessible. Some *medressahs*, the theological colleges attached to major mosques, are sometimes open to tourists. Trekking in the mountains, exploring the deserts, skiing in the High Atlas, deep-sea and trout fishing, hunting wild boar and duck-shooting are all available in addition to every kind of water sport. Tennis is popular and there are golf courses in Tangier, Agadir and Marrakesh. Kew Gardens has identified 375 species of wild flower in one valley alone! On the main migratory path, Morocco is the place to observe storks, flamingos, eagles, kingfishers, hoopoes, lapwings and roller bee-eaters.

FACT FILE

Money   The currency is the dirham (dh. or dr.), which it is illegal to import or export. Keep a few bank receipts, as proof of exchange, in case you need to reconvert dirhams on departure. Brisk exchange of sterling, traveller's cheques in banks. Credit cards accepted in larger hotels and retail outlets. No ATMs.

Travel documents   A valid ten-year UK passport is required. Travellers who plan to spend more than three months in Morocco must apply for permission at the police headquarters in any regional capital within fifteen days of arrival. A formality, but you may be required to prove that you can support yourself.

Circulation of traffic   Right-hand side. International road signs.

Electricity supply   220v AC. Round two-pin plugs.

Television and radio   One TV channel is in French.

Newspapers and books   No local English-language newspapers, but half the Press is French. Librarie des Colonnes, Blvd. Mohamed V, Tangier, has an excellent selection of English and French books. Paperback blockbusters in large tourist hotels.

Time difference   GMT in the winter.

Drinking water   Safe in the cities, though heavily chlorinated. Mineral water available.

Inoculations   None for the cities. Typhoid, cholera, hepatitis A and malaria prophylaxis may be necessary for treks to remote places. Take advice.

Medical assistance   Most doctors and dentists are French-speaking. Ask at the hotel or tourist office for English-speaking practitioners.

Language   French and Arabic are the two official languages and signs appear in both. English is widely spoken in the service industries, but the ability to speak French is a social asset.

Politics   'A constitutional and presidential monarchy.' Parliament is partly elected and has some powers. Left-wing and fundamentalist opposition.

Religion   Muslim. Synagogues and Roman Catholic churches in large towns (Mass usually in French). St Andrew's Anglican church in Tangier; Evangelical Protestant church in Agadir (services in English, French and German).

Shopping bargains   Leather goods, Berber rugs, fossils and semi-precious stones, marquetry, chased copper, inlaid silver, pottery.

Film   Print and slide film available. About £6 a roll.

Miscellaneous   Respect Muslim modesty by avoiding shorts and suntops in the streets. It is rude to point fingers or feet at others. 'Hassling' has given Morocco a bad name in recent years. The unofficial guides or 'students', who fasten on to tourists on arrival in Tangier or at the entrance to the souks in Marrakesh, are usually harmless, but they can be most tiresome. They soon recognize long-term residents and leave them alone. Until then, walk resolutely and refuse their services politely, but firmly. They are not without humour: 'Better one mosquito to bite you than a swarm!' they say. An official guide or a conducted tour arranged through the hotel or tourist office is often the best defence. The problem does not arise outside Tangier and Marrakesh. The hassle is easier to bear if you try to take a sympathetic view. With 50 per cent of the population under twenty-one and over 20 per cent unemployment in the cities, these young men at least wash and press their jeans, pick up a dozen languages (they are reputed to launch out in Basque or Finnish when the occasion demands!) and try to earn a few desperately needed dirhams. They do not sit in the streets with begging bowls. Some are really nice boys and, if you choose carefully, you may get a great deal of help at little cost.

Useful addresses

Moroccan National Tourist Office, 205 Regent Street, London W1R 7DE, Tel: 020 7437 0073.

Moroccan Embassy, 49 Queens Gate Gardens, London SW7 5NE, Tel: 020 7581 5001.

British Embassy, Blvd. de la Tour Hassan, Rabat, Tel: (37) 238600.

British Consulate, Rue d'Angleterre, Tangier, Tel: 93 5895.

Hon. British Consul, Hotel Sud Bahia, Rue des Administrations Publiques, Agadir, Tel: 841809.

British Council, 36 rue Tanger, Rabat.

PORTUGAL

Bounded on two sides by the Atlantic Ocean, Portugal is a lush green wooded land with a temperate climate. Only one area enjoys a reasonably warm winter and that is the Algarve, the dry southern coastal strip, which is protected from the north winds by its mountain ranges. It is a rocky coast, 150 miles long, with golden beaches sheltering under high cliffs. Its forested slopes and nature reserves are wonderful walking country. More genteel than the Spanish Costas, it has long been a favourite year-round destination for the British.

Climate

Maximum and Minimum Temperatures

Oct	Nov	Dec	Jan	Feb	Mar	Apr
22	19	16	15	16	18	20
16	13	10	9	10	11	13

High season   June to September.

Mid season   February to June. September to November.

Travelling there   Flights to Faro from Heathrow, Gatwick and provincial airports. Many cheap charters. Trains via Lisbon to Lagos and Faro. Weekly Eurolines service from Victoria Coach Station (46 hours). Motorists can cut down driving-time by taking a ferry to Bilbao or Santander in northern Spain.

Travelling around   Good bus services. Car, motorcycle and bicycle hire.

Travelling abroad   Spain. Morocco via Algeciras or Gibraltar.

Where to stay   Despite its small area, the *Algarve* has four quite distinct regions. The seaside tourist trade is concentrated along the central coastal strip between Lagos and Faro. Picturesque cobbled fishing villages have been extended to take in neighbouring beaches until they almost merge into one seamless, wall-to-wall resort. West of Lagos, the Sotovento (windward coast), is a fascinating area, dominated by the Fort of Sagres, where Henry the Navigator founded his school of navigation in the great fifteenth-century days of Portuguese exploration. On Cabo de São Vicente, four miles away, a lone lighthouse withstands the gales of Europe's most south-westerly point. This is wild, windswept country. East of Faro, the Barlavento (leeward coast) is an area of rich farmland and fig, citrus and almond groves. It is now joined to Spain by the recently completed bridge over the River Guardiana. With its national forest and the flamingos, storks and small waders of the Castro Marim nature reserve, this end of the Algarve is the place for nature-lovers. The inland area has old villages with a distinct Moorish feel, the renowned spa of Caldas de Monchique and beautiful mountain walks among the pines, chestnuts, cork-oaks and eucalyptus. There are orchids in the limestone regions and a profusion of wild flowers, as well as fifty-two species of bird. But it can be cold and wet in the mountains, when the weather on the coast is dry and sunny.

Lagos, from which the sixteenth-century caravelles set out to chart the sea-routes to India, is a historic city with elegant shops and good tourist facilities. Pleasant in itself, it makes the ideal base for exploring the Sotovento and the mountains of the Serra de Monchique. Those who prefer a real seaside resort could try neighbouring *Praia da Rocha* or *Portimão*.

Along the Barlavento Coast, *Tavira* is one of the oldest and most gracious towns in the Algarve. A seven-arched Roman bridge spans the Gilão River, while Moorish and Renaissance-style buildings overlook its public gardens.

Inland, there are good hotels and restaurants in *Monchique, Alte* and *São Bras*, but day trips to walk in the mountains in fair weather are probably preferable to residence in the winter.

Accommodation   Tourism is the Algarve's main industry and its highly developed resorts have the whole range of accommodation from five-star, luxury tourist complexes to modest pensions.

The coast between Lagos and Faro is in thrall to the international tour operators and hoteliers. There is little point in trying to go it alone, when a long-stay winter package on half board in a three- or four-star hotel can be obtained for as little as £125 a week per person, including flights and transfers; about £50 a week per person for self-catering in an aparthotel. Some packages include membership of the local golf club and/or free rounds of golf, which is a considerable saving. For those who prefer to be independent, the most suitable stretch of the Algarve is the eastern end, the Barlavento. This area is still relatively untouched by the package trade and you might be able to negotiate reductions of 25 to 50 per cent on long winter stays.

Starter hotel

Princesa do Gilgão, Rua Borda d'Agua de Aguiar 10, Tavira.
A comfortable small hotel in the town centre, overlooking the river. €42 for a double room (£28).

Nightlife   Everything from discos to darts in the resort hotels. Casinos at Vilamoura, Alvor and Monte Gordo.

Food   Sangres is the centre for lobster fishing and Tavira for tuna, but all the resorts offer freshly caught fish, *caldeirada* (fish stew), *ameijoas à Cataplana* (clams with pork) and *bacalhau* (the dried, salted cod for which there are said to be 365 recipes!). Excellent game, fruit and vegetables. Cakes and sweets made of almonds, eggs and sugar really *are* sweet. There are palatable local wines, the chief red wine of the Algarve being Lagoa. Portuguese cuisine relies on fresh ingredients, flavoured with herbs and simply cooked.

Tourists and expatriates   British tourists are the largest national group in the Algarve, followed by the Germans. Many now own properties there, some in the large residential complexes of the central Algarve, others in the area behind Tavira.

Leisure activities   Five hundred years of Moorish domination have left their imprint on the Algrave and its architecture. The Moors followed Phoenicians, Greeks and the Romans, who first planted the vines and generally organized the region. Fifteenth-century grandeur, eighteenth-century town planning at Vila Real de San Antonio and the remains of castles and monasteries offer a surprising amount of historical interest for so small an area. Walking and wildlife (See *Landscapes of Portugal: Algarve*, Sunflower Books, for detailed itineraries), game fishing, sailing, tennis. There is a Rambling Club at Albufeira. Portugal has made a speciality of golf; there are no fewer than thirteen golf courses in the Algarve, some of international championship standard. The Portuguese Tourist Office has detailed information. Bridge clubs; a weekly whist drive at Vilamura. The church at Loulé is very active.

FACT FILE

Money   The currency is the Euro, divided into 100 cents. No problem with sterling, traveller's cheques, or credit cards. ATMs in cities.

Travel documents   A ten-year UK passport gives entitlement to 90 days' stay. Extensions on application to the local police.

Circulation of traffic   Right-hand side. International road signs.

Electricity supply   220v AC. Round two-pin plugs.

Television and radio   Portuguese language only.

Newspapers and books   The *Portugal Post* and six Algarve newspapers and magazines. English paperbacks in resorts.

Time difference   GMT with no seasonal time change.

Drinking water   Tap water is safe. Plentiful mineral water.

Inoculations   None required.

Medical assistance   Many English-speaking doctors and dentists. Free emergency out-patient treatment available to British citizens under reciprocal arrangements.

Language   Portuguese. The people do not appreciate being addressed in Spanish, but English is widely spoken.

Politics   Republic with an elected president. Unicameral government elected by proportional representation. A member of the EC and NATO.

Religion   Roman Catholic. The International Evangelical Church of the Algarve, based at Loulé, has no building and moves around the resorts.

Shopping bargains   Leather shoes and handbags, embroidered linen, lace, hand-decorated glazed tiles (*azulejos*).

Film   All types and brands available, at roughly UK prices.

Useful addresses

Portuguese National Tourist Office, 22/25a Sackville Street, London W1X 1DE, Tel: 020 7494 1441.

There are tourist offices in all the resorts.

Portuguese Consulate General, 62 Brompton Road, London SW3 1BW, Tel: 020 7581 3598.

British Embassy, Rua de São Bernardo 33, P-1249-082
   Lisbon. Tel: (21) 392 4000.
British Consulate in Portimão.

SPAIN

The south-east coast of Spain is deservedly one of the most
popular winter destinations. Inland, the high Sierras are snow-
covered for much of the year and a thirty-mile drive up into the
mesa will take you from the warm beaches and orange groves of
the Mediterranean to the equivalent of the Pennines in January.
The Atlantic coast (Costa de la Luz) is cool and breezy. The best
sunshine, as the name suggests, is to be found on the Costa del
Sol.

THE COSTA DEL SOL

Facing south across the Mediterranean and sheltered from the
north winds by the mountains of Andalucia, the Costa del Sol
enjoys a remarkably clement winter climate. Certain resorts
along its golden, sandy coastline have been over-developed for
some tastes; but there are still miles of deserted beach and wild,
gorse-covered heathland for those who like quieter pleasures.
Leisure facilities are excellent and the cultural treasures of
Southern Spain and Morocco are within easy reach. There is
something for everyone along the Costa del Sol – and 320 days
of sunshine every year.

Climate

Maximum and Minimum Coastal Temperatures

Oct	Nov	Dec	Jan	Feb	Mar	Apr
23	19	17	16	16	18	20
16	12	9	8	9	11	13

High season May to October, but the winter is becoming
increasingly popular.

Travelling there Fly to Malaga or Gibraltar, take the train or
drive. For those who can cope with thirty-six hours on a bus,
there is a weekly Eurolines coach service from Victoria to

Algeciras, calling at all the Costa del Sol resorts on the way. Lots of budget flights.

Travelling around   Granada, Seville, Cordoba, Cadiz, Jerez and Gibraltar are all an easy bus ride away.

Travelling abroad   Frequent daily car ferries from Algeciras and Gibraltar to Morocco (Tangier and Ceuta). Ferry from Malaga to Palma de Mallorca. Buses into Portugal.

Where to stay   Those who like what the holiday brochures term 'lively' resorts will make for *Torremolinos, Fuengirola* and the slightly quieter *Benalmadena Costa* with its nudist beach, all within a few miles of Malaga. Here they will live in comfort in modern tower-block hotels and apartment blocks, with swimming pools and an excellent range of facilities. English pubs and fast-food outlets will provide a familiar background, while the seafront cafés will show British television programmes to their British clientèle.

For those who like town life, but prefer something a bit more Spanish, *Malaga* itself has a certain charm, with its smart shops, its orange and jacaranda trees and its shady walks through the botanical gardens.

Marbella is sliced in two by the terrifying N340, the coastal motorway which bypasses the other resorts. But the picturesque old town, set back from the road, is a haven of tranquillity and the beach area is well developed. There are expensive and elegant shops, as befits the most up-market of the Costa resorts.

Going further west, *Estepona* is a quiet little Spanish town which happens to be on the sea, rather than a developed resort. Its clean beach and shady promenade, and the cafés along the seafront, are patronized by the Spanish. There are no hamburger-joints. A few miles beyond Estepona in the Sottogrande direction, the tourists disappear altogether and travellers with a taste for solitude can enjoy the spectacular coastline undisturbed.

Accommodation   The major tour operators have taken over Torremolinos, Fuengirola and Benalmadena Costa. If you are looking for half board in a three- or four-star hotel, or self-catering in a well appointed aparthotel, you cannot do better on price than buy a long-stay package. Depending on the firm and the number of stars, these can cost as little as £105 a week per person for half board in a hotel and around £50 a week per person for self-catering, including the cost of the flights and transfers.

Malaga, Marbella and Estepona are still possible destinations for the independent traveller. Pensions and two-star hotels in Spain are of a very acceptable standard and there are, of course, plenty of five-stars at the top end of the market.

Starter hotels

Hostal El Cenachero, calle Barroso 5, Malaga. A quiet, comfortable hotel, just off the seafront. €36 for a double room (£24).

Hostal La Pilarica, calle San Cristobal 31, Marbella. A quiet hotel overlooking a flower-lined street. €48 for a double room (£36).

Those looking for bargain accommodation in Marbella should check out the old town, where the *hostals* start at around €30 (£20) a room.

Hostal El Pilar, overlooking the charming Plaza Las Flores, Estepona. €36 for a double room (£24).

Use Estepona as your base to explore the coastline towards Sottogrande, where small hotels and pensions perch on cliff-tops overlooking clean, deserted beaches. Good bus services.

Note: *Do not be put off by the word Hostal. It is the usual Spanish word for a hotel and has nothing at all to do with our hostels.*

Torremolinos, Fuengirola and Benalmadena Costa are not really interested in the independent traveller and most hotels are unwilling even to discuss reductions for long stays. But expect to negotiate at least 25 per cent off in Malaga, Marbella, Estepona and the small coastal pensions.

Nightlife The usual pubs and discos in the major resorts. Elsewhere, the Spaniards tend to dine late and their dinner is their nightlife. They stroll the streets and window-shop long after most tourists have gone to bed.

Food The package hotels offer English breakfast and a self-service buffet dinner, which is basically English with a little dash of Spanish. Dining out is still relatively inexpensive. The favourite breakfast is *churros*, hot fresh-fried doughnuts the size and shape of chipolata sausages, served with hot chocolate. Excellent sea-food, paella, pork chops, salad and fruit, though the Spaniards are a little over-fond of the frying pan and meals can be heavy. A huge variety of *tapas* (small snacks) and *bocadillos* (sandwiches) stave off hunger until the late evening meal. Excellent sherry and table wines. Good beers.

Tourists and expatriates The Costa del Sol has more tower-blocks and more whitewashed, red-tiled village developments than the rest of Spain put together and thousands of elderly British residents recline on their terraces in the shade of their satellite dishes. Add the winter tourists and the market in Fuengirola is more like Liverpool on a Saturday morning than anywhere in Spain. If you want British company, the resorts near Malaga are the ones to choose. Spain begins west of Marbella.

Leisure activities Phoenicians, Greeks, Romans and Arabs held this coast. Inland, at Granada, Seville and Cordoba, are some of the most spectacular Moorish buildings in the world, the legacy of Spain's conquest by the Muslims. And Spanish baroque is in a league of its own. Those interested in history and the arts will find ample occupation for a whole winter. (Take warm clothes for trips into the interior.) There are sixteen splendid golf courses. Tennis is well provided for and there is walking, swimming for the hardy, fishing and hunting (September to mid-February: licence needed). The tourist hotels offer chess, boules, billiards, cards, aerobics and rifle-shooting. Skiing in the Sierra Nevada.

VALENCIA

Those who enjoy the vitality and cultural amenities of a significant city might try Valencia, which is far enough south and sufficiently sheltered to have mild, sunny winters. Not over-large or over-noisy, it is easily explored on foot. There is real charm and elegance in its small squares with their wrought-iron balconies and lanterns, its fountains splashing in the shade of the trees and its old streets with their high door-knockers (at hand's reach to callers on horseback). Its status as a university city offers cultural possibilities; a fine cathedral, chapels, one of the richest art collections in Spain, museums, cinemas and arcades of fine shops provide occupation for the occasional rainy day. Situated midway between Barcelona and Alicante, it is a good base from which to explore the Costas and the Roman cities of Sagunto, Tarragona and Tortosa. Ferries cross from Valencia to Mallorca and Ibiza.

Starter hotel

Hotel La Marcelina, Paseo de Neptuno 72, Valencia. Near the sea and recently refurbished to a high standard. €36 for a double room (£24).

There is a Eurolines coach service to Valencia, via Avignon and Barcelona; train services and direct flights from London. 25 per cent reductions on long-stay hotel prices should be possible.

THE BALEARIC ISLANDS

Like all islands, the Balearics are breezy. This makes them agreeably cool in summer, but produces some real cold snaps in winter. Minorca, in particular, which is a flat island, offers no leeward shelter from the *tramontana*, the winter wind from the north. Ibiza and tiny Formentera, the smallest islands in the group, have a milder climate along their sheltered southern shores, but virtually close down in the winter. This leaves Mallorca, the largest and most popular island for holidaymakers.

Mallorca's mountains protect the spectacular sweep of Palma Bay, dominated by its towering Gothic cathedral. This is the part of the island to choose, as the rest of the coast and the flattish centre are exposed to the winter winds. The major tour operators have taken over here and there is little point in trying to go it alone, when a long winter stay on half board in a three- or four-star hotel can be bought for as little as £90 a week per person, including the flights and transfers. Self-catering deals in aparthotels start at around £60 each, based on two sharing. The packages offer the full range of evening entertainments, from sequence dancing to bingo, and often include discount vouchers for the eight golf courses, which can be a considerable saving.

There are over 15,000 resident Britons on Mallorca. There are English-language newspapers, a British Club in Palma and an Anglican Church. Palma is a winter 'home from home' with the added advantages of a reasonably good climate, excellent walking in the Sierra de Tramontana (see *Landscapes of Mallorca*, Sunflower Books, for detailed walks) and the old towns of Palma, Andraitx and Roman Pollensa for the historically-minded to explore. Ferries to Valencia, Alicante and Barcelona open up the possibility of short trips to the mainland. Mallorca is not all fish and chips and lager, but has considerable charm, particularly in the quieter winter season.

Climate

Maximum and Minimum Temperatures

Oct	Nov	Dec	Jan	Feb	Mar	Apr
23	18	15	14	15	17	19
14	10	8	6	6	8	10

High season   May to October.

FACT FILE

Money   The currency is the Euro, divided into 100 cents. Sterling, dollars and traveller's cheques are easily exchanged; credit and charge cards accepted. ATMs in cities.

Travel documents   A full UK ten-year passport gives entitlement to a 90-day stay. Extensions on application to the local police before the end of the 90 days.

Circulation of traffic   Right-hand side. International road signs.
Electricity supply   220v AC. Continental plugs with two round pins.
Newspapers and books   English-language newspapers published locally include: the *Reporter*, Malaga (monthly), the *Sur*, Malaga (weekly), the *Marbella Times* (monthly), the *Costa del Sol 'What's On'* (monthly), the *Majorca Daily Bulletin*, the *Iberian Daily Sun*. More are free from Tourist Offices. Valencia has good bookshops with English books. Resort towns stock popular paperback fiction.
Time difference   GMT + 1 or 2 hours, depending on the time of year.
Drinking water   Tap water safe, unless the local reservoir is low. Plentiful mineral water.
Inoculations   None required.
Medical assistance   Enquire at the hotel or tourist office for English-speaking doctors and dentists.
Language   Castilian (standard) Spanish dominates in the regions included here. English is widely spoken.
Politics   Spain is a constitutional monarchy, a member of the EC and NATO.
Religion   Devoutly Roman Catholic, with many centres of pilgrimage and religious feast days. Some Protestant churches and synagogues in large cities and resorts.
Shopping bargains   Leather and suede. Inlaid wood and metalwork of Moorish design. Embroidery.
Film   Print and slide film available, at roughly British prices.
Useful addresses

Spanish Tourist Office, 23 Manchester Square, London W1. Tel: 020 7486 8077.

Spanish Consulate General, 20 Draycott Place, London SW3 2SB, Tel: 020 7581 5921.

Consulates in Edinburgh and Manchester.

British Embassy, Calle Fernando el Santo 16, Madrid, Tel: (91) 700 8200.

British Consulates in Malaga and Palma de Mallorca.
There are helpful Tourist Offices, well signposted, in every
Spanish town.

TUNISIA

Tunisia is the most developed country in North Africa, with a
high standard of living and high levels of literacy. Free health
care has brought infectious diseases under control and there is
even a social security system. Everything is done to make the
visitor's stay safe and comfortable, as the country relies heavily
on tourism. Seven hundred miles of white sandy beach, golf
courses, olive and citrus groves, oases, delicious food, hotels of
every category, Roman ruins, Islamic architecture and a friendly,
polyglot population all contribute to the interest and vitality of
this small country. It is deservedly popular as a year-round
holiday destination.

Climate

Maximum and Minimum Southern Coastal Temperatures

Oct	Nov	Dec	Jan	Feb	Mar	Apr
27	22	17	16	18	21	23
17	11	7	6	7	9	12

Night temperatures fall to 4° inland, in the Sahara.

High season   May to October.

Travelling there   The three international airports at Tunis, Djerba
and Monastir are used throughout the year for scheduled and
charter flights. Car ferries from Marseille, Trapani and Catania
(Sicily), Cagliari (Sardinia) and Genoa.

Travelling around   A few good trains. The national bus company
(SNTRI) operates air-conditioned coaches between cities, which
connect up with regional bus services. Car hire is relatively
expensive, but the long-distance taxis (louages), which take five
passengers and leave when full, are a convenient alternative.
Four-wheel drive vehicles and guides needed for the desert.

Travelling abroad   Ferries to France and Italy.

Where to stay   Tunis and the Cape Bon resorts on the north coast are vulnerable to winter winds and rain. It is necessary to go south, to the sheltered Bay of Hammamet and beyond, to be sure of clement weather.

Hammamet, Sousse and *Monastir* have the highest concentrations of winter holidaymakers. Although Hammamet is little more than a string of tourist hotels along a sweep of palm-fringed beach, Sousse and Monastir retain some character, with their medinas, kasbahs, ramparts and ninth-century mosques. Sousse has a good mosaic museum and the oddity of the main Tunis to Sfax railway running unfenced down the centre of the high street!

For those who like the vitality of a city, Tunisia's second largest, *Sfax*, has modern hotels in the new town, which the French built beside the medina, and a good climate. The centre of a communications network, it is an excellent base from which to explore the interior and the oases of the South. *Mahdia*, just south of Monastir, used to be the capital of the Fatimid rulers and is now a charming small resort with good bathing, a shady cobbled old town within the medina walls, a silk museum and a few fishing boats.

Djerba, reputed to be Homer's Island of the Lotus Eaters, has been a pleasure resort since Roman times. Joined to the mainland by a causeway, it does not have the claustrophobic feel of some islands. Ancient walled towns, fishing villages, modern resorts, palms, olives, figs, pomegranates and apricots – the island has everything. For an easy-going, yet interesting, stay Djerba would be a very good choice.

Tunisia has tamed the Sahara and built luxury hotels in its oasis cities. 'Roughing it' is quite unnecessary and those who like it really hot and dry might even consider spending a winter among the date-palms. In *Nefta* and *Tozeur*, the most developed resorts, sand-yachting competes with camel-riding, hot springs, palaeontology and Berber traditions. In *Matmata*, where the Berbers have traditionally lived in caves to protect themselves from the heat, modern hotels of great character have been excavated from the rocks. Tozeur would be the best base for exploration.

Accommodation   Tunisia has every class of hotel from self-contained four-star de luxe tourist complexes on the beach to flophouses in the medinas. They are inspected and categorized by the Government and must display their tariffs at reception.

Those wanting three- or four-star accommodation in Hammamet, Sousse, Monastir or Djerba would be advised to book a long-stay package through a tour operator, as their prices can work out as low as £85 a week per person on half board, including the flights and transfers.

For those who prefer a little more contact with the Tunisians, the one- and two-star hotels are generally clean and well run. Some excellent value, cheaper hotels, run by the Touring Club de Tunisie, are converted fondouks (caravanserais) and traditional houses. Matmata even has underground hotels!

Starter hotels

Hotel el Mehdi, Mahdia. A spacious hotel with indoor and outdoor swimming pools and tennis courts. TD40 for a double room with breakfast (£21).

Hotel des Oliviers (3-star), Ave. Hahib Thameur, Sfax. A gracious old building with a swimming pool. TD 40 for a double with breakfast (£21).

Hotel Continental (3-star), Ave. Abdulkacem Chebbi, Tozeur. A modern hotel with a palm-shaded swimming pool. TD 50 for a double with breakfast (£26).

Reductions of 25 to 30 per cent should be possible on a long stay.

Nightlife   The package-tour hotels offer everything from discos to dominoes, with occasional sorties for traditional Berber evenings, belly-dancing displays or performances of *malouf* music on the lyre, violin and tambourine. There are discos in the main resorts, but sitting outside the cafés and restaurants is the main evening occupation.

Food   Though bland international food has infiltrated the more popular resorts, real Tunisian food is a subtle blend of French and North African. Croissants, brioches and authentic *cuisine française* compete with local *brik* (a flaky pastry triangle stuffed with egg, parsley and onion) and *couscous* (a bed of steamed grain semolina covered in any kind of meat, fish or vegetable stew). The seas are rich in Mediterranean fish, including lobster. The local beers and some Tunisian wines are quite palatable. *Boukha* (fig brandy), *Thibarine* (a liqueur) and *lagmi* (palm sap) are local specialities. Mint tea is the national beverage.

Tourists and expatriates　British tourists are thick on the ground in the larger resorts, but few own property there.

Leisure activities　Homer's Lotus Eaters, Virgil's Queen Dido, Hannibal and the Roman legions were followed by Arabs, Spanish, Turks and French, none of whom managed to crush the indigenous Berbers. Tunisia has some of the finest Roman sites in the world, at Dougga, Bulla Regia, Thuburbo Maius, El Djem and Sbeitla, and the collection of Roman mosaics in the Bardo Museum, Tunis, is outstanding. Kairouan, with its great seventh-century mosque, is Islam's fourth holiest city. Fossils in the desert and traditional Berber crafts add extra dimensions to the historical and artistic interest of the country. Monastir and Hammamet have 18-hole golf courses. There is riding, tennis, every kind of water sport, parascending and sand-yachting. Lac Ichteul is the winter refuge of spoonbills, geese, ducks and wagtails and it is on the migratory path for swallows, warblers and birds of prey. There are one hundred spas with thermal springs, many run by medical staff.

FACT FILE

Money　The currency is the Tunisian dinar (TD), divided into 1,000 millimes. Sterling and traveller's cheques can be exchanged at banks or hotels. Credit cards widely accepted. The dinar is not convertible and must be bought on arrival in Tunisia. Keep some currency receipts, as you may need them to reconvert any remaining dinars on departure. ATMs in resorts.

Travel documents Full British ten-year passport gives entitlement to three months' residence. Extension on application to the local police station. You are advised to report there early in your stay, as the extension may take some time to process. There is a fine of TD 45 (about £30), payable on departure, by those who have overstayed without permission.

Circulation of traffic Right-hand side. International road signs.

Electricity supply 200v AC, though some smaller towns in the Sahara are still on 110v. Round two-pin plugs.

Television and radio French programmes on both, as well as Arabic.

Newspapers and books No local English-language newspaper, but half the Press is French. Shops stock French books, but English literature is scarce, apart from the latest paperback blockbusters in tourist hotels.

Time difference GMT + 1 hour October to April.

Drinking water Bottled water advised.

Inoculations None.

Medical assistance Doctors and dentists likely to be French-speaking. Ask at hotels and tourist offices for English-speaking practitioners.

Language The two official languages are French and Arabic. English is widely spoken in the service industries, but ability to speak French is a social asset.

Politics A presidential Republic. An elected Chamber of Deputies with an executive president.

Religion Tolerant Islam. The Tunisians have a relaxed attitude towards alcohol and visitors are allowed inside mosques. Historic Jewish communities. Roman Catholic churches in Tunis; St Joseph's Mission in Monastir; Sfax Chapel.

Shopping bargains Berber rugs (classified by quality and Government labelled), pottery, Kairouan leatherwork, beaten copper and brass, Hand of Fatima jewellery, sand roses.

Film All types and brands available, but slightly more expensive than in the UK.

Useful addresses

Tunisian National Tourist Office, 77a Wigmore Street, London W1H 9LJ, Tel: 020 7224 5561.

There are Tourist Information Offices in all major Tunisian towns and resorts.

Tunisian Embassy, 29 Prince's Gate, London SW7 1QG, Tel: 020 7584 8117.

British Embassy, 5 Place de la Victoire, Tunis 1000. Tel: (7) 34 1444.

TURKEY

The Mediterranean coast of Turkey is one of the most beautiful in the world, its small harbours, sandy beaches, orange groves, vineyards and spectacular historical sites protected from the harsh winter climate of Central Anatolia by the snow-capped Lycian and Taurus Ranges. There are hotels and pensions to suit every pocket and the food is delicious. The Turks are genuinely hospitable people, who are much more inclined to invite visitors into their homes than other Mediterranean folk. The lifestyle is Western, with a dash of the Middle East to give it spice. Those adventurous enough to try something a bit different will be richly rewarded.

Climate

Maximum and Minimum Daily Temperatures for Izmir – the nearest available.

Oct	Nov	Dec	Jan	Feb	Mar	Apr
24	19	14	13	14	17	21
13	9	6	4	4	6	9

Temperatures on the more sheltered Mediterranean coast are usually 2° or 3° higher.

High season   May to October.

Travelling there   Fly to Istanbul and change for Antalya or Dalaman. If you can stand a twelve-hour coach journey, do as most Turks do: fly to Istanbul, take a taxi or service bus to the bus station (*otogar*) and catch an express coach for a fascinating journey across the snow-bound Anatolian plateau. No need to book in advance.

Travelling around   Excellent coach services along the coast, or for longer excursions inland. Taxis are cheap and the dolmuş (shared taxi) even cheaper. Self-drive cars and scooters.

Travelling abroad   Winter ferry services from Marmaris to Rhodes and from Mersin and Silifke to Turkish Cyprus. (Embarkation tax of about £32 on passengers returning from Rhodes to Marmaris.) Overland to Greece and Syria, but your Syrian visa must be obtained beforehand, in London.

Where to stay   For winter living, avoid the areas set aside for tourist development, as these die off out of season. Choose instead a thriving Turkish community, where there is considerable local life throughout the year. *Antalya*, the chief city of the Mediterranean coast, is an excellent choice. From its central position, it offers unrivalled access to places of interest and, although it has all the modern amenities, it has not lost the flavour of its historic past. For those who like something a little quieter, *Marmaris* is an attractive town built around its yacht marina and surrounded by wooded hills. It is a favourite resort of wealthy Turks from Istanbul and Ankara, who ensure that standards of comfort and service are maintained. It is rather out of the way, down its peninsula, but that is part of its charm. *Kaş* is probably the best choice for those who favour village life. In the winter the men return to their fishing and the women refurbish their pensions ready for the next season. But the open-air market does a brisk trade and the restaurants are still open. Its coastal situation is stunningly beautiful and it is a good centre for exploration.

Accommodation   Antalya and Marmaris have the full range of hotels, from five-stars as luxurious as any in Western Europe to simple pensions. The best hotels in Kaş are less grand, but still of a good standard. Whatever level of accommodation you require, a little footwork and much haggling (without which no Turkish deal is complete) will produce excellent bargains. Expect to negotiate reductions of 35 to 60 per cent.

Antalya is an extensive city and the five-star hotels are self-contained worlds out at the seaward end of its large bay, in Lara and the boulevards leading to it. The heart of the city is the maze of winding, cobbled streets running down to the old harbour, now an elegant yacht basin, with the boulevards and shopping areas behind. This is the area to be, as the Turks themselves live and work here and there is a cheerful buzz of activity. A number of good three-star hotels line the main boulevards, but the greatest concentration of hotels is to be found around the old harbour. Many are sixteenth-century Ottoman merchants' houses, built in traditional style round a courtyard with orange trees. Imaginatively converted, they are furnished with white pine and Turkish rugs. The views over the marina are spectacular and the south-facing rooms are suntraps, but check that there is heating at night.

As in Antalya, the four- and five-star hotels of Marmaris are out of town, along the bay in the Içmeler and Turunç direction, a dolmuş ride from the centre. But there are hotels in all the other categories in the town itself, their relative price depending partly on their proximity to the seafront boulevard and marinas. None of the hotels in Kaş is officially rated higher than 2-star, but Tourist Ministry standards are exacting and the hotels are clean, with private facilities. There are real bargains in winter. Many family-run pensions offer double rooms for as little as Tl. 30,000 a night (£2.50). As Kaş is a small fishing village, everything is within walking distance.

Starter hotels

Otel Grand Maryot, Kazim Ozalp Cad., Antalya. A smart new hotel in the pedestrianized town centre. Large double rooms with TV and minibar.

Otel Ayşe, 64 Sokak 11, Marmaris. A quiet, comfortable family-run hotel with a small swimming pool.

Korsan Karakedi Motel, Kaş. In a quiet street behind the hospital, the motel has a roof terrace with splendid views and a bar.

Note: *No prices are quoted, as the Turkish lira is in free fall. I recently stayed in the Grand Maryot, the plushest of the three recommended hotels, for around £6 a night, including breakfast – and that was for a short stay. The long-stay rate should be even lower.*

Nightlife   Dining out. A few international hotels run discos and belly-dancing displays for tourist groups. Casino at Marmaris.

Food   Turkish cuisine is one of the world's finest and it is worth going to Turkey just to eat! Seasonal vegetables, salads and fruits, charcoal-grilled meats, kebabs, fresh fish, interesting casseroles and crisp bread served straight from the oven provide an endless variety of healthy eating. The national drink is *raki*, a clear aniseed-flavoured grape spirit (Greek *ouzo*). Good wines and beers. Tea is drunk without milk in small tulip-shaped glasses. Try the refreshing apple tea (*elma çay*) and morello cherry juice in mineral water (*vişne suyu*). In the smarter restaurants the waiters speak English; in the more homely *lokantas*, it is the custom to go into the kitchen to choose.

Tourists and expatriates   Southern Turkey is not the place to go if you need an English social life, though British tourists in the winter constitute the third largest group after the Germans and French. Antalya, in particular, has seen a marked increase over the past two or three years. There are a few British residents in apartment blocks and village developments along the coast, particularly in the Marmaris and Fethiye areas; Antalya has British people working in the travel offices and schools. Marmaris has so many British living on board their yachts in the marina that an Hon. British Consul has his office there.

Leisure activities   Lycians, Greeks, Romans, Byzantines, Seljuks and Ottomans have all left their monuments along the coast and those with an interest in history will find occupation for more than one winter. Visit the magnificent Roman theatre at Aspendos, the rock-tombs of Demre, the huge Seljuk castle at Alanya and the fortress city of Termessos, perched dizzyingly on its crag. Take an excursion coach, or simply catch a local bus and ask to be put down at the nearest point, so that you can walk to the ruins through the pine woods, or across the fields of wild cyclamen, asphodel and thyme. Excursions inland to Konya (the whirling dervishes), Pamukkale's hot mineral baths, Izmir and Ephesus. Seven new golf courses have been constructed in Antalya Province. Fishing, boat-trips, sea-bathing for the hardy. For walks, see *Landscapes of Turkey, Antalya and Marmaris*, Sunflower Books. Turkish baths. There is a nature reserve at Dalyan. Backgammon (tavla) is the Turkish passion and a good way to make friends with the locals.

FACT FILE

Money   The currency is the Turkish lira (Tl). Inflation is rampant, so money should be changed in small amounts. Sterling and traveller's cheques are all accepted at banks and post offices, but few retail outlets take credit cards. ATMs in cities.

Travel documents   A ten-year UK passport and a visa. £10, paid in sterling at the point of entry into Turkey, buys a three-month visa. Extensions from the nearest police headquarters.

Circulation of traffic   Right-hand side. International road signs.

Electricity supply   220v AC. Round two-pin plugs.

Television and radio   Daily news bulletins in English.

Newspapers and books   The *Turkish Daily News*. A few novels, set for school examinations, in the book shops. Paperbacks in large resort hotels. The Owl Book Shop in Antalya runs a book-exchange.

Time difference   GMT + 2hours.

Drinking water   Tap water is safe in towns. Mineral water plentiful.

Inoculations   None required for this region of Turkey.

Medical assistance   Many doctors and dentists are Western-trained. Ask the hotel or tourist office for an English-speaker. Payment necessary.

Language   Turkish is fiendishly difficult, but the effort to learn a few words is greeted with delight. Roman script. English is spoken in the service industries and many country people speak German, as they have worked in German factories.

Politics   The Turkish Republic is a unicameral parliamentary democracy, with wide presidential powers. A member of NATO and an aspiring member of the EC.

Religion   Muslim, though Turkey is a secular state guaranteeing freedom of worship to non-Muslims. The nearest active Christian churches and synagogues are in Izmir. The fifth-century Byzantine church of St Nicholas at Demre holds an International Santa Claus Symposium every year on 6 December.

Shopping bargains   Leather and suede goods, carpets, copper, bronze, onyx, alabaster, honey.

Film   Slide-film difficult to find. All film is expensive, at about £8 a roll.

Miscellaneous   Nodding the head up and down means 'Yes', as in England, but the sideways shake means 'I do not understand'. 'No' is a backward toss of the head, often accompanied by 'tsk'. Blowing the nose and kissing in public are considered offensive. As it is a Muslim country, decorum in dress is appreciated. Shoes should be removed and women should cover their heads when visiting mosques. Women may go virtually everywhere, but an unescorted man may not go into parks, restaurants, etc. marked 'Aile'. These are reserved for women and family groups. Old-fashioned sawdust-floored tea-houses, thick with the smoke of hookahs, are best left to the men.

Useful addresses

Turkish Tourist Information Office, 170/173 Piccadilly, London W1V 9DD, Tel: 020 7629 7771.

There are tourist offices in all main Turkish resorts.

Turkish Consulate General, Rutland Lodge, Rutland Gardens, London SW7 1BX, Tel: 020 7589 0949.

British Embassy, Şehit Ersan Cad. 46a, Çankaya, Ankara,
Tel: (312) 455 3344.
Hon. British Consuls in Antalya and Marmaris.

FURTHER AFIELD

AUSTRALIA

Australia is the world's largest island. Steamy, tropical Northern Queensland is as near to the Equator as Angola or Peru, while Victoria lies in the sunny, temperate 30s. It spans three time zones. Although it is roughly the same size as the USA, its population is only 17.5 million as compared with America's 255.5 million. Most people live along the south-east coastal strip from Adelaide to Cairns, or the western strip around Perth. The centre of the country, where the 150,000 Aboriginals live, is very sparsely populated and this vast empty outback begins where suburbia ends. Despite the recent recession, Australia still enjoys a high standard of living. The developed coastal strips would be expensive places to spend a whole winter, especially as our winter is Australia's summer season. Add to the cost of high-season accommodation the considerable cost of the fares, and Australia is attractive only to those who have relations with whom they can stay, those with large resources, or those who are heading for the campsites and stations of the outback. There are some package holidays, but they are all of limited duration.

Climate

Maximum and Minimum Daily Temperatures

Sydney (South East)

Oct	Nov	Dec	Jan	Feb	Mar	Apr
22	23	25	26	26	24	22
13	16	17	18	18	17	14

Darwin (North West)

Oct	Nov	Dec	Jan	Feb	Mar	Apr
34	34	33	32	32	33	33
25	26	26	25	25	25	24

Alice Springs (Centre)

Oct	Nov	Dec	Jan	Feb	Mar	Apr
31	34	36	36	35	32	27
14	18	20	21	21	17	12

Cairns (North East)

Oct	Nov	Dec	Jan	Feb	Mar	Apr
30	31	32	32	32	31	29
20	21	23	23	23	23	21

High season

   Temperate southern states: October to April.

   Tropical North: Hot and dry March to October. Hot and wet
     November to February.

School holidays and companies' annual leave: Mid-December to
end of January.

Travelling there   Flights to all major destinations, including
the new international airports at Cairns and Brisbane. Fares
are highest in our mid-winter, but shop around for bargains. Most airlines include a Far East stopover in the price.
It is worth considering a round-the-world ticket, as these
can be obtained for as little as £100–£150 extra and include
a number of stopovers out and back. An experienced firm,
such as Cooks or Trailfinders in Earls Court, will help you
through the maze of possibilities. Going by sea can cost as
much as you choose, or it can be quite economical. P.&O.
fares, for example, begin at £4,010 for forty nights at sea;
top prices around £30,000. Or there are passenger-carrying
cargo boats which offer cheaper rates (see Round-the-World
Cruises).

Travelling around   Special air, train and coach passes are
available, giving discounts of up to 50 per cent on normal fares.
Many tours, including camping tours, safaris and special interest
travel, may be booked locally or before departure.

Travelling abroad   New Zealand, Indonesia, Papua New Guinea,
Polynesia, South Pacific.

Where to stay   This will depend entirely upon your interests, the location of relations or friends and the degree of heat you can stand.

Western Australia, with its dynamic city of Perth, is the wealthiest part of the continent. It has a spectacular coastline and national parks. In the south, rich farmland and vineyards flourish in its Mediterranean climate; but its wealth comes from the vast mineral resources of its scorching deserts and the Kimberley Plateau in the north. Nearer to Indonesia than to Sydney, it has a young, self-reliant population and an exciting frontier feel, but it is too remote to be a convenient base for touring.

The Northern Territory, which includes coastal Darwin, Alice Springs and Ayers Rock, the world's largest megalith, is a spectacular region for a visit, but probably too hot for most people to spend our winter there. The same applies to Northern Queensland, which is wet and steamy at that time of year, while the dangerous stinging box jellyfish infest the Queensland coast from November onwards.

So most visitors during this period settle for the East – the cities and resorts along the beautiful sandy Pacific Coast, which stretches north to Southern Queensland and the Great Barrier Reef (too far out to sea for the jellyfish). *Sydney, Brisbane* and *Melbourne* are all delightful cities. If you prefer somewhere quieter, there are excellent resorts all along the coast, connected to the south of Sydney by the Princess Highway and to the north by the Pacific Highway. With Sydney or Brisbane as your first base, you could travel along the coast until you found your perfect winter retreat. Moving up the coast from the south, *Nowra, Batemans Bay, Narooma* and *Merimbula* all have their charms. North of Sydney there are the long, lonely beaches, some with spectacular surf, around *Newcastle*. *Port Macquarie*, the main resort, is a pleasant town, as are *Coffs Harbour* and *Grafton* with its November Jacaranda Festival. The Gold Coast, just south of Brisbane, is highly commercialized and crowded in high season, but the Sunshine Coast to the north still has some secluded beaches. The resorts and island around *Cairns* are sophisticated take-off points for the Great Barrier Reef. Mountain ranges tower behind most of these resorts, while the Queensland beaches are backed by rainforest and tropical fruit farms.

As Australia is so vast and offers so many possibilities, those without contacts over there really need the advice of a knowledgeable travel firm and/or the Australian Tourist Commission. They will help you to devise a programme adapted to your personal interests and the travel agent will make your initial bookings.

Accommodation In addition to the usual range of hotels, aparthotels, motels and guest houses, Australia has many bed and breakfast establishments and also homestays on working farms. For those who wish to live really economically, the excellent Youth Hostel network is open to all ages, and there are reasonably priced cabins at campsites. Four- and five-star hotels begin at around A$ 250 (£95) a night for a double room, while the cheapest budget accommodation in, say, the King's Cross area of Sydney can be as low at A$ 30 (£11 a night) – if you can find it in the high season and if you are brave enough to stay in this nightlife district! You get what you pay for. Surcharges are common at weekends and during holiday periods.

Starter hotels The popular Flag Chain operates a discount voucher scheme throughout its five hundred hotels and motels, with prices ranging from £74 for a double in the Silver Star grade establishments down to £32 for a double in their cheapest, Yellow Grade hotels. Rooms in all grades have private facilities, tea- and coffee-making equipment, refrigerator, colour TV, radio, telephone and central heating or air conditioning. If you are not going out to friends and are not booking your first nights' accommodation through a travel agent, a few Flag vouchers, pre-paid in the UK, will solve all your problems. Information from your travel agent, or direct from Flag (UK telephone 020 7808 5666), who will send you a free Flag Directory and make an initial booking for you in the destination of your choice.

Motorhomes   Like the USA, Australia is great touring country. Those who enjoy driving might consider renting a Motorhome, for economy combined with maximum freedom and flexibility. In December and January the rates are currently around £51 a day for five weeks or more in a standard two-person camper, falling to about £35 from mid-January to the end of March. Four-wheel drive campers cost another £30. Unlimited mileage, transfers to and from the airport, insurance, maps and advice are all provided free of charge. Bookable in advance through Cooks and other large travel agents.

Nightlife   Discos, jazz clubs, pubs, casinos, or the sedater pleasures of dining out. Bars are still male preserves, where serious drinking takes place.

Food   Australia is no country for the vegetarian. Roast meats, steaks, barbecues, sausages and meat pies form the traditional diet. For the bold, there is even kangaroo meat, camel, buffalo, crocodile and wichetty grubs (moth larvae). Excellent fresh fish and seasonal vegetables. Tropical fruits and fruit juices. Post-war immigration from the Mediterranean, the Middle East and Asia has enlivened the local cuisine and there is a wide variety of ethnic restaurants in all the major cities. Australian wines have a deservedly high reputation – and for the thirsty, there is always the famous amber nectar!

Leisure activities   The Sydney Opera House and the excellence of recent Australian film-making have put the continent on the cultural map. Every city has its historical museum, its theatres, cinemas and botanical gardens. But most visitors go to Australia for the outdoor life on the beaches, the spectacular coral reefs and the vast, red outback. There is everything from camel-trekking to shooting the rapids and bungy jumping. Less strenuous activities include game fishing, sailing, golf and bush-walking with experienced guides. And for spectators, there is the cricket season. The Australian Tourist Commission has special brochures for each sporting activity.

FACT FILE

Money   The currency is the Australian dollar (A$), divided into 100 cents. No problem with currency, traveller's cheques or credit cards. ATMs in towns.

Travel documents   A ten-year British passport and a visa. Visitors' visas are issued free of charge and are valid for six months. For young people interested in working their way around there is a special twelve-month working visa.

Circulation of traffic   Left-hand side. International road signs.

Electricity supply   240/250v AC. Flat three-pin plugs, but different in design from those in the UK.

TV and radio   All local stations broadcast in English.

Newspapers and books   English-language Press. British newspapers take some time to arrive and are expensive.

Time difference   Western Time – GMT + 8 hours. Central Time – GMT + 9½ hours. Eastern Time – GMT + 10 hours.

Drinking water   Safe in towns. Plentiful mineral water.

Inoculations   None required.

Medical assistance   Excellent and only moderately expensive, but insurance is still recommended. Beware of sunburn and sunstroke.

Language   English, with its own wide and picturesque vocabulary: 'arvo' for afternoon, 'station' for farm, 'yakka' for work. Known as 'Strine', the language requires some study. (Try to get hold of *Strine* by Afferbeck Lauder. Failing that, the Lonely Planet Guide to Australia has a good vocabulary list.)

Politics   A federal commonwealth within the British Commonwealth, with a Governor General representing the Queen. Bicameral parliamentary democracy, in which the prime minister is the leader of the party with the largest number of seats in the House of Representatives.

Religion   Places of worship for every religion in this multi-cultural country.

Shopping bargains   None. Good buys are handknits, sportswear, opals, pink diamonds.

Film All types and brands readily available at roughly UK prices. Stock up in Singapore if you are making a stopover there.

Miscellaneous Tipping is not common, except in expensive restaurants, where 10 per cent is expected – though even here Australians may leave only A\$ 3 or 4.

It is considered offensive for a person travelling alone in a taxi to sit in the back. Australians are fiercely egalitarian and 'tall poppies' are soon cut down to size.

Useful addresses

Australian Tourist Commission, Gemini House, 10/18 Putney Hill, London SW15 6AA, Tel: 020 8780 1424.

Branches of the ATC in all major Australian cities and resorts, as well as State tourist offices. Excellent literature.

Austravel are the booking experts. 61 Conduit Street, London W1S 2GB, Tel: 0870 166 2120. Branches in Birmingham, Bournemouth, Bristol, Edinburgh, Leeds and Manchester.

Australian High Commission, Australia House, Strand, London WC2B 4LU, Tel: 020 7379 4334.

British High Commission, Commonwealth Avenue, Canberra ACT 2600. Tel: (2) 6270 6666.

British Consulates in Brisbane, Melbourne, Perth and Sydney.

BRAZIL

Everything about Brazil is larger than life. In area it is greater than the USA. The Amazon is the world's mightiest river, with 1,100 known tributaries, 20 per cent of the world's fresh water and an estuary over 200 miles wide. There are 5,000 miles of superb palm-fringed beach along the Atlantic Coast, as well as the white sandbanks of the great rivers, many with their hotels and pleasure resorts. Brazil has 30 per cent of the world's remaining tropical forest, some of it still unexplored, with the richest and most diverse ecosystem on our planet. It has the Iguaçu Falls, greater than either the Niagara or the Victoria, throwing rainbows of water in 275 magnificent cascades of more than 250 feet. It has the world's largest wetlands, in Pantanal, with the greatest concentration of fauna in South America, from its 200 species of bird to alligators, anacondas and the rare, shy jaguar. It has Portuguese sixteenth- and seventeenth-century colonial cities, where the churches are covered in gold, the altars are solid silver and the architecture unbelievably extravagant. It has Rio, carnival, the samba, the bossa nova and football-mania. In sum, Brazil is a land of unimaginable natural beauty, with a joyous, exuberant lifestyle dedicated to pleasure. And as South American states go, it is relatively stable politically.

But it is not a land for the faint-hearted. If you are not daunted by the scale of everything, you may be distressed by the absolute poverty in which one-quarter of the population lives. The slums (*favelas*) round the major cities are notorious for their squalor, and disease is rife there. In tourist areas, you need to be vigilant night and day, as petty theft is a way of life. But for those who take proper medical precautions and watch over their possessions, Brazil offers luxury at comparatively low cost, a beautiful climate and enough occupation for a dozen idyllic winters. And as the Amazon Basin is being settled, lumbered and sadly depleted, now is the time to see it, before the exploiters have finished their savage depredations.

Climate

Rio de Janeiro

Maximum and Minimum Daily Temperatures

Oct	Nov	Dec	Jan	Feb	Mar	Apr
26	28	28	30	30	27	29
20	20	22	23	23	23	21

Salvador da Bahia

Oct	Nov	Dec	Jan	Feb	Mar	Apr
28	28	29	29	29	29	28
22	23	23	23	23	24	23

Manaus (up the Amazon)

Oct	Nov	Dec	Jan	Feb	Mar	Apr
33	32	31	30	30	30	30
24	24	24	23	23	23	23

Seasonal changes are less significant nearer to the Equator. The rainy months are:

Rio	October to March
Salvador	March to July
Manaus	All the year, with lighter rainfall from August to October.

High season December to February, when the Brazilians are on holiday.

Travelling there BA and Varig (Brazil's international airline) fly direct from London to many major cities; TAP flies via Lisbon and Air France via Cayenne in French Guyana. Shop around for discounted fares. Though many economy fares have a three-month limit, it may actually work out cheaper to discard the return half and buy a single back home. The Holland America Line operates cruise ships to Salvador, and there are cargo ships from London, Tilbury and Hamburg, to Rio, Salvador and Recife. For details, including connecting flights, consult The Cruise People Ltd (see under Round-the-World Cruises).

Travelling around Varig, Vasp and Transbrasil have extensive flight networks. Fares are high, but air passes, purchased outside Brazil, give reductions over a two- or three-week period. The air-taxis (*teco-teco*) are best avoided for safety reasons. Excellent, inexpensive bus services of two classes: the *leito* or *executivo* bus costs twice as much as the *comum*, travels at night and has fully reclining seats, with blankets and pillows. Rivers are major highways with every kind of boat from large liners to dug-outs. Taxis are moderate in price, but agree the fare first if there is no meter. The major international car rental firms have branches throughout Brazil, with prices similar to those in the UK. Payment must be made by credit or charge card.

Travelling abroad Brazil is bounded by Argentina, Bolivia, the

Guyanas, Paraguay, Peru, Surinam, Uruguay and Venezuela.

Check the visa requirements with the appropriate Consulates in London before departure.

Where to stay *Rio de Janeiro* may well be your port of entry and it is a spectacular city, which deserves at least a week of your attention. But our winter is their rainy season and the humidity there can be oppressive. Above all, avoid Rio from December to February, when the holidaymaking Brazilians are so thick on the sand that it is almost 'standing room only' on the famous Copacabana and Ipanema beaches. My own base for exploration would be further north-east along the coast, where there is less humidity at that time of year and the heat is tempered by tropical breezes.

Those who like to be in, or near, a major city will find *Salvador da Bahia* one of the most exciting and joyous places they have ever had the good fortune to visit. From the moment when Amérigo Vespucci sailed into the bay on All Saints' Day, 1501, and called it Baia de Todos os Santos, until 1763, Salvador was the capital of Brazil. The sumptuous cathedral and the large number of splendid sixteenth- and seventeenth-century churches, convents and noble houses of its colonial quarter are evidence of its historical importance. The manual elevator, installed by the Jesuits in 1610 to take them up and down from the city centre (*Cidade Alto*) to the bay (*Cidade Baixa*) has been replaced by efficient electric lifts, so that it is easy to live in the middle of past glories and yet enjoy the pleasures of a seaside life. The beaches near Bahia are clean and white. Ride in the bus out of town for fifteen or twenty minutes and take your pick – deserted, palm-fringed coves or lively beaches with restaurants, bars and water sports of every description. Salvador is the centre of Afro-Brazilian culture. The fusion of Catholicism with African religious cults has produced *candomblé, macumba* and *umbanda*. The Church festivals are lavish and spectacular, especially that of Senhor Bom Jesus dos Navagantes on New Year's Eve, when the procession winds down to a beach alive with music, al fresco

restaurants and bars. And Carnival in Bahia is world famous –
less commercialized than Rio and accompanied by the music of
the local *trios electricos*. Music is a way of life there and you will
gradually get used to the easy-going, laid-back style of the
people. It is Brazil's second most popular tourist destination, so
keep an eye on your possessions.

If you like a quieter, less multicultural place, *Maceió* is hard
to beat. North of Salvador and south of Recife, it is a friendly
modern city with a few interesting old colonial buildings. The
turquoise sea lapping its superb white beaches is sheltered by a
coral reef, and there is a lagoon for boating and wildlife
watching. Cheerful walkers and joggers throng the promenades
in the early mornings; and in the evenings the small shrimp and
fish restaurants along the shore do a brisk trade under the stars.
Carnival there is more intimate and therefore safer than the
carnivals in major cities, and December has its own Festa do Mar
(Festival of the Sea). At weekends, wandering musicians and
entertainers weave in and out of the seaside handicraft stores,
while the cavalry parades by on splendid Manga Larga
Marchador horses. With its perfect climate and low cost of living,
Maceió is Lotus Land, where you could hitch your hammock to
a couple of coconut palms and laze for ever in the sunshine.

Both Salvador and Maceió are centrally situated along the
Atlantic coast with good communications. Using either as your
home, you can travel with relative ease up to the north and west,
to Belém and Manaus in the Amazon Basin, south to Rio, and
inland to the Iguaçu Falls, the Pantanal Wetlands and other
national parks. These are all fascinating areas to explore, but
better for a visit than as a long-term winter base. There are more
creature comforts in the coastal towns, where two-thirds of all
Brazilians live.

Accommodation   Hotels are categorized by EMBRATUR, the
Brazilian tourist authority, and cover the whole range from one
to five stars. The regulated price must be posted on the wall in
every bedroom. The smarter hotels are as smart as anything in

Europe. Cheaper hotels are often called *pensãos* or *pousadas*. There are *quartos* (without private facilities) and *apartamentos* (with private facilities). Aparthotels are popular in cities and good value for money.

For travel in remote areas without hotels, the Amazon or the north-east, for example, take a hammock and a sleeping bag and find shelter with friendly locals, who may or may not charge you a dollar or two. A hammock is also useful on all but the most luxurious air-conditioned Amazon steamers, as it is often preferable to travel *secundo* and sleep in a hammock on the deck than to swelter in a cabin in *primeiro*. Avoid motels, where rooms are rented out by the hour, complete with ceiling mirrors! Motels in Brazil are used for accommodation only when nothing else can be found.

It is virtually impossible to quote current, meaningful prices, as inflation skyrockets and prices are out of date before the printer's ink is dry. Tariffs are normally quoted in dollars, rather than reals, and are modest by our standards. If you are moving around to popular destinations between December and February, or during Carnival, it is best to book ahead, as accommodation may be difficult to find. No reductions can be expected then, but you should be able to negotiate a 20 per cent reduction on a long stay at other times. Because of inflation, expect a rising scale rather than a fixed rate.

Starter hotels

Hotel do Pelourinho, Rua Alfredo de Brito 20, Cidade Alta, Salvador. A former mansion in the heart of the old town. Courtyard with palms, bananas and parrots. Good restaurant and fine harbour views.

Hotel Europa, Itapoa. A friendly hotel on the beach, a short bus ride north along the coast from downtown Salvador. Itapoa is an old fishing village, a small resort in its own right, with a range of hotels, restaurants and food stalls along its beautiful sands.

Pousada Rex, Rua Dr Antonio Pedro de Mendonca 311,

Maceió. Just 50 m from the sands, the hotel's pleasant rooms surround a shady courtyard. English-speaking owner.

Note: *As the real is in a volatile state, it is difficult to quote meaningful prices, but you should not expect to pay more than £10 a night for a double room, and you will often pay much less.*

In Salvador, Bahiatursa (offices at Praça Tomé de Souza, Palacio Rio Branca, the airport and the bus station) have an efficient accommodation service. They make placements in private houses as well as in hotels.

Nightlife   Salvador is the musical capital of Brazil. Whereas Rio has only the samba, Salvador has absorbed, transformed and made its own a diversity of styles from Africa and North America. There is music and dancing in the cafés and bars; and cultural groups, mostly black, rehearse their political numbers outside their clubhouses. But while gringos may dance in the bars, they should not go to the clubhouses unless invited and escorted. Unfortunately, it is asking for a mugging to stroll the streets at night. Take a taxi to and from your restaurant.

In Maceió the evenings are quieter, but there are craft stalls along the well-lit seafront, and the seafood restaurants and simpler food stalls do a brisk trade.

The seafronts of both cities are cheerful and well lit, with plenty of good restaurants.

Food   The Atlantic Coast has an exotic cuisine, a mixture of African, Indian and European – fish and shellfish, hot peppers cooked in palm oil, dendé oil or coconut oil with fresh coriander. If there is a national dish, it is *feijoada*, a meat stew served with rice and beans. Steak, chicken and fish are plentiful. Snacks are usually small pies (*empada, empadina, esfiha*) stuffed with shrimp, chicken, beef, cheese or palm-hearts. *Churrasco* is spit-roasted meat taken in a *churrascaria*, where you eat as many cuts as you can manage. Brazil is no place for the vegetarian! Wonderful tropical fruits. Good beer, mediocre wine. The local spirit is *cachaça*, a sugar cane rum. Soft drinks are plentiful and cheaper than mineral water. Try *guaraná*, the local variety, as a change from the ubiquitous cokes. Really strong black coffee with plenty of sugar is the national beverage.

Tourists and expatriates   Tourists are mostly Australasians and Americans, with a sprinkling of Europeans, mostly from the Mediterranean countries which settled the land. Few British have migrated to Brazil. In Salvador there is a British Club, Inglesa 20B, and Cultura Inglesa, Rua Plinio Moscoso 357; the Associacão Brasil-Estados Unidos, Av. 7 de Setembro 1883, has a library and reading room open to all.

Leisure activities   Portuguese settlement and the power of the Jesuits produced a string of sixteenth- and seventeenth-century architectural gems all the way up the coast from Rio to Belém. The seventeenth-century gold rush was responsible for the sumptuous inland city of Ouro Preto and the rubber boom at the turn of the last century for Manaus on the Rio Negro, a city of legendary wealth hacked out of the jungle, opera house and all. Gross inequalities in the distribution of wealth provide the visitor with the whole range of cultural possibilities in music and the arts, from excellent concerts by international orchestras to the impromptu music of the streets and *favelas*. The beach is a way of life for Brazilians of all classes and shades of colour. For the naturalist, Brazil is without equal anywhere on our planet. Those who might be interested in joining scientists as volunteers on ecological projects should write for a free information pack to Earthwatch, Belsyre Court/TT, 57 Woodstock Road, Oxford, OX2 6HU (Tel: 01865 311600). They have over 400 teams currently engaged in research and conservation work worldwide, including rainforest projects. A minimum commitment of two weeks is required.

FACT FILE

Money   The currency is the Brazilian real, divided into 100 centavos. As the economy teeters on the edge of hyperinflation, rates of exchange are noticeably different from day to day, so money should be changed in small quantities. It is essential to take US dollars and dollar traveller's cheques, preferably American Express, though Thomas Cook, Barclays and First National City Bank are also recognized. Dollars (and dollars only) may be exchanged at the tourist rate (dolár turismo), which can be twice as high as the official rate (dolár oficial), at which all other currencies must be exchanged. The black market rate (dolár paralelo) is better than either and is sometimes offered at tourist shops, travel agents and exchange bureaux. Do not be tempted by street black-marketeers. Cash dollars are highly prized and therefore most useful throughout the country – but they are also dangerous to carry. Credit and charge cards are accepted in the cities and there are now some ATMs. Keep a few exchange receipts, in case you wish to reconvert on departure.

There are currently no limits on the import and export of currencies by tourists. The money situation is highly complex and will probably have changed completely by the time this book appears in print. Amazingly, people do seem to manage, and goods and services are bought and sold in Brazil as freely as elsewhere. But it is essential to study the prevailing rates and currencies before making major purchases.

Travel documents   A full ten-year British passport and an onward or return ticket (or evidence of sufficient funds to buy one). A 90-day visa will be issued on entry into Brazil and this may be extended for another 90 days at the visa section of the federal police station in any state capital. Apply at least 15 days before the expiry of the first visa. You will be required to produce the carbon copy of your entry card when you leave the country. Failure to do so may result in a $100 fine.

You are legally obliged to carry your passport at all times. A tourist passport, bought from the accommodation desk at Rio Airport, is said to be an acceptable alternative, which enables you to leave your real passport in the hotel safe. Have at least one photocopy of your passport details hidden away in your luggage.

It is illegal to enter Brazil as a tourist and undertake paid work.

Circulation of traffic   Right-hand side. International road signs. Road fatalities are high and pedestrians regarded as fair game.

Electricity supply   110v AC or 220v AC. Two-pin round plugs. Exercise caution with electrical appliances, especially electric showers.

Television and radio   Portuguese only. Cinemas usually show films in the original English with Portuguese sub-titles.

Newspapers and books   The *Latin American Daily Post* and the *Miami Herald*. American newspapers in the major cities. In Salvador, the Livraria Brandão, Livraria Civilizacão Brasiliera, Graúna and Livraria Planeta stock both new and second-hand English books.

Time difference   East Coast: GMT – 3 hours. Interior: GMT – 4 hours. Far West: GMT – 5 hours.

Drinking water   Do not drink tap water unless you know that it has been treated. *Água gelada*, the chilled water put on the tables in good restaurants and hotels, is usually filtered or boiled. Plentiful mineral water and bottled drinks.

Inoculations   Yellow fever and malaria prophylaxis for Amazonia. Hepatitis A. Take your yellow WHO vaccination certificate with you. Take up-to-date advice from the experts (see Chapter 8). Do not bathe in lakes or slow rivers, which are breeding grounds for dire snails and parasites.

Medical assistance   The Rio Health Collective (24-hour telephone answering service on 325 9300 ex.44) will put you in touch with an English-speaking doctor, as will tourist offices and large hotels. Always take your own new needle with you if you need an injection. Avoid blood transfusions and immunoglobulin inoculations against hepatitis, as screening for AIDS is unreliable. If you need blood, consult the nearest British Consulate or get yourself repatriated.

Language   The Brazilians are proud of being the only Portuguese-speaking people in South America. Spanish is usually understood, but not appreciated; Italian is more acceptable. English is widely spoken in the tourist areas, but a little Portuguese is essential up-country.

Politics A fragile democracy, with an elected president. A powerful militia stands by and takes over from time to time, but the régime is generally more liberal than many in South America. Brazil has provided a haven over the years to political refugees from the military dictatorships in Argentina, Chile and Paraguay.

Religion Brazil has the largest Roman Catholic population of any country in the world. African cults brought over by the slaves are powerful forces, either openly in the magical, sacrificial ceremonies of *umbanda, candomblé* (performed in the Yoruba language) and *quimbanda* (a banned black magic cult), or syncretically, in the secret identification of Catholic saints with African gods. The influence of some Indian religions has spread to other sections of the population, especially in the Brasilia region. The more superstitious Brazilians see nothing wrong in attending mass in the morning and participating in candomblé at night. Tourist Offices can sometimes arrange visits to one of the *terreiros* to witness a ceremony.

Shopping bargains Jewellery, gems and semi-precious stones, especially amethyst. Leather goods. Handicrafts in tropical hardwoods, basketware and pottery. Guitars, other stringed and percussion instruments. Cigars.

Film Film, cameras and photographic accessories are all very expensive. Take a good stock of film. A modest model of camera is less of an invitation to theft.

Miscellaneous A one-page fax, sent from a main post office, is cheaper than an international phone call. Tipping is 10–15 per cent, but agree the fare in advance with taxi-drivers and do not tip. Suntan lotion is hard to find and expensive. High fashion reigns on the beaches. Buy your swimwear in Brazil, or be scorned as an antediluvian gringo. Carry only the money you need for the day, plus a few extra dollars to satisfy potential robbers. They are often quite gentlemanly and will let you keep enough money for your fare back to your hotel if you ask. Never resist robbery. It is better to lose your dollars than your life.

Useful addresses

Brazilian Embassy, 32 Green Street, London W1Y 4AT, Tel: 020 7499 0877.

Brazilian Consulate General, 6 St Albans Street, London SW1, Tel: 020 7930 9055.

There is no Brazilian Tourist Office in London, but some information may be obtained from the Brazilian Trade Centre at 32 Green Street. Tel: 020 7499 0877.

Branches of EMBRATUR and individual State tourist offices in major cities and resorts in Brazil.

British Embassy, SES, Quadra 801, Conjunto K, CEP 70.408–900, Brasilia, DF.

British Consulates in Rio and Salvador.

THE CANARY ISLANDS

Lying off the north-west coast of Africa, washed by the Gulf Stream and cooled by the NE trades and the Atlantic westerlies, this semi-tropical archipelago enjoys permanent spring weather. The climate is so temperate that there is no need for either central heating or air conditioning.

The thirteen islands, spread over 250 miles of ocean, are all different from one another. The Eastern Group (largest islands Gran Canaria, Lanzarote and Fuerteventura) are like their Saharan neighbour, with scanty or no rainfall and an arid landscape, surprisingly splashed with green. The Western Group (Tenerife, Palma, Gomera and Hierro) have volcanic peaks which catch the rain-clouds from the Atlantic and are lusher in vegetation. But even within each island there are different climates, the northern and western coasts being rainier and greener than the eastern and southern.

The landscape of all the islands is exotic: black lava beaches, snow-capped extinct volcanoes rising out of banana plantations, strings of camels crossing black desert moonscapes, where walls of lava protect the vines and fig trees from the high winds, and some of the lushest, rarest vegetation in the northern hemisphere. Travellers must study the climate of these distinctive islands and choose the one which suits them best. And sun-worshippers must be sure to choose a resort on the hotter drier side. It is claimed that there are no snakes, mosquitos, tarantulas or even flies on the islands!

Climate

Maximum and Minimum Temperatures

Oct	Nov	Dec	Jan	Feb	Mar	Apr
26	24	22	21	22	22	22
19	18	16	14	14	15	16

High season   Winter.

Travelling there   Direct scheduled and charter flights from many UK airports. There are airports on all the islands except Gomera.

Travelling around   Each island has its bus services. Ferries and regular flights between the islands.

Travelling abroad   No accessible neighbours.

Where to stay   The most developed islands for tourism are Tenerife and Gran Canaria, with Lanzarote catching up fast.

Tenerife, a gem of an island, has long been a favourite of the British. *Puerto de la Cruz* on the northern coast is an elegant resort of hibiscus, palm trees and botanical gardens – the compensation for its occasional rainy days. *Los Christianos* and *Playa de las Americas* on the southern coast have nothing but desert behind them, but they do have guaranteed sunshine, golden sand imported from the Sahara and a younger, livelier nightlife. There is something for everyone on Tenerife and it would be my first choice.

Gran Canaria, one of the Eastern Group, is drier and hotter, with sweeping sand-dunes along its shores and pine forests in its mountainous centre. *Sioux City*, where the Spaghetti Westerns are made, small towns with the houses of the Conquistadors and the major port of *Las Palmas* add variety. Most tourist development is in the sunny south, at *Playa del Ingles, Maspalomas* and *Puerto Rico*.

Lanzarote, the Fire Island, has no underground water and virtually no rainfall. It is a landscape of extinct volcanic craters and black lava, raked by the wind. Travellers either love it or hate it. Resorts are mostly on the sunny southern shore, around the capital, *Arrecife*, and the airport – the *Costa Teguise, Matagorda, Playa de los Pocillos* and *Puerto del Carmen*. Quieter to date than Tenerife and Gran Canaria, Lanzarote has avoided some of their mistakes, rejecting tower-block hotels in favour of development more sympathetic to the landscape.

The smaller islands of La Gomera, La Palma, Hierro and Fuerteventura have some limited hotel accommodation, but the difficulty of getting supplies over to them makes the cost of living higher. Each has its attractions, but I doubt if they would be great enough to last a whole winter. Those with a longing for solitude would be advised to make a reconnaissance from a base on one of the larger islands before committing themselves to a winter's isolation.

Accommodation   The larger islands are in thrall to the tour operators. If you wish to stay on Tenerife, Lanzarote or Gran Canaria, it is difficult to find your own accommodation, as the hotels are booked solid for groups; even the small back-street pensions have contracts with German and Scandinavian budget companies. Long-stay packages in three- or four-star hotels start at around £150 a week per person, half board; £120 per person self-catering. These prices include flights and transfers. As winter is high season, there are no real bargains and it would not pay to try to go it alone. A few hotels offer 5 per cent off on a long stay, but cannot guarantee a room throughout the season. Unless you are looking for five-star accommodation, which is always available, a package is really the only possibility.

Nightlife   Nightspots run the whole gamut from sedate and sophisticated in Puerto de la Cruz, Tenerife, to the lager and disco end of the market. Sequence dances, whist drives, bingo and Happy Hours in package hotels. Seafront cafés and bars, where it is pleasant to linger in the evening over coffee and a liqueur.

Food   Canarian specialities are found in the local restaurants, not in the tourist hotels, where the food is generally ample, but bland. *Sancocho* (a rich fish stew), *conejo salmorejo* (rabbit in a piquant sauce), *papas arrugadas* (literally 'wrinkled potatoes', salty and boiled in their skins) and *mojo*, the accompaniment to most meat and fish dishes. Red mojo is made of sweet red peppers and chilli, while green mojo is milder, with a parsley and coriander base. Deep sea fish and shellfish abound; the bold will try *sepia*, the local cuttlefish. Spanish *tapas* and *bocadillos* (snacks and sandwiches) in the cafés, and there are even hamburger and pizza parlours. Wines are mostly Spanish, as the Canarian grape harvest produces only small, and therefore expensive, vintages. Good local beer.

Tourists and expatriates   Tenerife has long been a favourite with the British, who constitute the largest winter tourist group. Many have bought apartments and settled there. In fact, English seems to be driving out Spanish as the local language and everything is reassuringly familiar. It is possible to lead an active English social life. The other islands have fewer British residents. The small island of La Palma has a colony of European escapists.

Leisure activities Mostly centred around the hotel swimming pools and tennis courts. Every kind of water sport, including surfboarding in the spectacular Atlantic rollers, though the ocean is chilly for bathing. Deep-sea fishing for tuna and barracuda. There are two golf courses on Tenerife, two on Gran Canaria and one on Lanzarote. Bowls, table tennis, scrabble, whist drives and bingo in the tourist hotels. Walking in the National Parks (see the Sunflower Books *Landscapes* series for detailed itineraries of walks on Gran Canaria, Lanzarote, Fuerteventura, La Gomera and Tenerife). Botany – there are over six hundred plants unique to the Canaries. Puerto de la Cruz on Tenerife has courses in Spanish language and culture and the Anglican Church there runs weekly whist drives and has a library. Organized excursions are expensive (at £25–£35 for a day trip) and worth the price only to ascend volcanoes or visit the more desolate areas; the local buses have wide networks and offer travel cards with discounts, so most resorts and beauty spots are easily accessible independently.

FACT FILE

Money   The currency is the Euro. Sterling, dollars and traveller's cheques are easily exchanged; credit and charge cards accepted. ATMs in resorts.

Travel documents   A full UK ten-year passport gives entitlement to a 90-day stay. Extensions on application to the local police before the end of the 90 days.

Circulation of traffic   Right-hand side. International road signs.

Electricity supply   220v AC. Round two-pin plugs.

Newspapers and books   No locally published English-language newspapers. Bookshops in most resorts sell light paperback fiction. An English library in Puerto de la Cruz, Tenerife, offers temporary membership.

Television and radio   All local transmissions in Spanish.

Time difference   GMT.

Drinking water   Tap water is safe. Plentiful mineral water.

Inoculations   None required.

Medical assistance   Hospitals and clinics are well equipped and have English-speaking doctors. Payment necessary.

Language   Spanish. English is spoken in all resorts, though some Spanish is required inland.

Politics   The Canary Islands constitute two provinces of Spain and are subject to Spanish law. They are not in membership of the EC, so the single-market relaxations in the import of dutiable goods do not apply.

Religion   Devoutly Roman Catholic. Puerto de la Cruz, Tenerife, has an Anglican church, All Saints, which runs a programme of social services and entertainments. Nuestra Señora de la Piedad

celebrates Mass in English. There are no synagogues or mosques.
Shopping bargains   Lace and embroidery of the highest quality,
but not cheap. Duty free liquors, cigars and cigarillos (tobacco
grown from Havana seed).
Film   Film for both prints and slides available. Price in
photography shops roughly the same as in England, but the
seafront stalls charge exorbitant prices.
Useful addresses

Spanish Tourist Office, 23 Manchester Square, London WI.
Tel: 020 7486 8077.

There are tourist offices in all the main Canarian resorts.

Spanish Consulate General, 20 Draycott Place, London
SW3 2SB, Tel: 020 7581 5921.

Consulates in Edinburgh and Manchester.

British Embassy, Calle Fernando el Santo 16, Madrid, Tel:
(91) 700 8200.

There is a British Consulate on Tenerife.

The Canary Islands have a special reduced-rate telephone
information service for tourists, in English, on Tel:
901 300 600.

INDIA (INCLUDING GOA)

India is overwhelming in its beauty and diversity. United under
the British Raj, it is a heady, fomenting brew of kingdoms,
religions, traditions, cultures and languages (fourteen of them,
with hundreds of dialects). Geographically, it encompasses the
Himalayas, the deserts of Rajastan, rainforest, mighty rivers and
thousands of miles of fine, silver sands under waving palm trees.
Whatever your interests, from mountaineering to snorkelling,
from temple sculpture to tiger-watching, your only problem in
this vast and varied land will be how to see and do it all in one
lifetime.

India is not a wholly comfortable country. The silks, spices,
jewels and palaces have poverty and the cardboard shacks of the
slums as their backdrop; and the stubborn bureaucracy of petty

officials, the noise, the dirt and the crowds can fray even the calmest nerves. At times, you will long to escape – but once back home, the vibrant colours, the roses and bougainvillea, the scent of jasmine, the smiles and the swish of silken saris in the dust will haunt you until you return.

Goa was a Portuguese colony until 1961. It offers its own particular blend of the familiar and the exotic and its palm-fringed beaches, washed by the Arabian Sea, are the perfect places for the cautious to dip in their toes. It would be possible to live comfortably in a European-style resort complex in Goa and have nothing at all to do with the real India, but that would be a missed opportunity. The Indians speak English and are kind to foreigners, so do venture forth from the enclave and experience some of the wonders, joys and frustrations of their magnificent land.

Climate

Goa

Maximum and Minimum Daily Temperatures

Oct	Nov	Dec	Jan	Feb	Mar	Apr
31	33	33	31	32	32	33
23	22	21	19	20	23	25

Monsoon June to October

Chennai (formerly Madras)

Maximum and Minimum Daily Temperatures

Oct	Nov	Dec	Jan	Feb	Mar	Apr
32	29	28	29	31	33	35
24	23	21	20	21	23	26

Monsoon July to December

High season   Winter, especially Christmas.

Travelling there   Flights by many international airlines to major Indian cities. Many excursion and cut-price fares, so shop around.

Travelling around   Indian railways are legendary (there are still some steam engines), slow, and comfortable in first class. Efficient, if sometimes ramshackle, buses. Internal flights are heavily subsidized. Taxis, chauffeur-driven cars and cycle-rickshaws are so cheap that car hire is unnecessary. For the locals, bicycles are the main form of transport and sturdy black sit-up-and-begs can be hired on every street corner. In Goa, there are wonderful old Enfields for hire by motorcycle enthusiasts.

Travelling abroad   India is one of the stop-overs on the Australasia routes. Burma, Thailand, Malaysia, Nepal, Pakistan and Bangladesh.

Where to stay   There is so much to see in India that it seems a pity to stay anywhere. But most of us like a base, where we feel at home and from which we can make expeditions. My two suggestions are both on the sea, but on opposite coasts and very different from each other in their culture and lifestyle.

Goa has in recent years become increasingly popular as a winter resort and it is easy to see why. A former Portuguese colony, it is in some ways a little bit of Europe on the Arabian Sea. The large Christian population worships in grandiose Portuguese Catholic churches, the cuisine has a flavour of Europe and the smarter hotels and beach complexes would do credit to any resort on the Algarve. Add silver sands, blue seas, guaranteed sunshine and a low cost of living, and you have the perfect choice for a winter escape.

Your only problem will be choosing your beach, as there are so many with excellent facilities. Those to the north of the state are on the whole more developed than those to the south, but all offer miles of clean, empty sand within a few minutes' walk of the resort centre. Now is the time to stay in Goa. The surrounding villages are already being deprived of water, so that the tourists may enjoy unlimited showers, and the fishermen are leaving the sea to become waiters. Without careful planning and controls, Goa could become the victim of its own success and another tropical paradise could be lost.

For those who like the cultural stimulus of a city, my own choice would be Chennai (formerly Madras), cooled by the breezes of the Bay of Bengal. The capital of the state of Tamil Nadu in the Hindu heartland, it is far away from the religious conflicts with the Muslims in the north and is a peaceful, spacious city with a distinguished past and a thriving present. Unlike Goa, it is mainstream India, but gently and charmingly so. The site of the East India Company's first settlement in 1639, Chennai grew from small beginnings at Fort St George to become India's fourth largest city. To the Georgian architecture of the port, the Victorians added their extravagant Indo-Saracenic Law Courts, post offices, stations, libraries and museums. There are Victorian Gothic churches. The Chennai Museum houses the country's finest collection of South Indian bronzes and Buddhist antiquities. There is the 1896 Connemara Public Library, the Chennai Literary Society, the Pantheon, the Archives and the Music Academy. In fact, there is so much cultural activity that you may occasionally have to flee to the perfect beaches nearby – and even here you will find seventh-century temples and exquisite Pallava sculptures on the beaches of Mamallapuram (formerly Mahabalipuram). Yet, although Chennai offers so many occupations for all tastes, it is still an easy-going city with friendly, relaxed people and some of the best food in India.

Accommodation

Goa   If you are visiting India for the first time, you may feel happier booking through one of the specialist long-haul agents, though you will pay dearly for the convenience. Most agents use the Taj Holiday Villages, which belong to India's most prestigious chain of hotels. Kuoni's prices start at £758 per person for a week on full board, including flights, transfers and all entertainments. Extensions by arrangement. Fear of flying and the unknown, post-September 11, have dealt a particularly hard blow to the exotic end of the travel market, and there is no reason why you should not state your own terms. It should be quite possible to book a week's luxury package, while you find your feet in Goa, then go off independently, having arranged with the travel agency in advance to defer your flight home. Look out for special deals too.

Those who go it alone are unlikely to negotiate better terms independently at the luxury hotels featured in the travel brochures. But there is plenty of other accommodation in every price bracket, most of it categorized by the Indian Government. Unless you have seen a seaside resort in the brochures which has made an immediate appeal to you, the best course is to start by taking a hotel room in Panaji (or Panjim). This small state capital on the River Mandovi is a pleasant town with whitewashed buildings, red-tiled roofs, bougainvillea and Portuguese churches. Buses, both regular and excursion, set off from there to run along the beaches and you can tour all the resorts and check out their hotels before choosing. Colva Beach and its quieter neighbour, Benaulim, are deservedly popular. Chapora has secluded sandy coves round a Portuguese fort. Calangute is larger and livelier. Sinquerim, near to Panaji, is where the major complexes are. The cheapest accommodation is usually a row of palm-roofed shacks attached to a beach restaurant and these can cost as little as £1 a night. A bungalow in a mid-range Government-owned Tourist Complex will cost in the region of £5–£8. There are literally hundreds of hotels, all competing for business, so consult the guidebooks and tourist offices, have a good look round, and haggle! You can expect at least a 25 per cent reduction on a long stay, with possibly a small supplement over Christmas.

Starter hotels

Hotel Delmon, C. de Alberquerque Road, Panaji. A clean, modern hotel with a useful business centre. From Rs.1200 for a double room (£16).

Broadlands Hotel, 16 Vallabha Agraharam Street, Chennai. A deservedly popular hotel, with rooms overlooking shady courtyards and helpful management. From Rs.400 (£6).

Hotel Kanchi, 28 C-in-C Road, Chennai. A modern hotel with rooftop restaurant. From Rs.800 (£11).

Note: *There is often a range of accommodation on offer within*

*each Indian hotel, from dorm beds to plush air-conditioned
suites, and you get what you pay for. Ask to see a selection of
rooms before deciding.*

In Chennai, the swimming pool and the old-world elegance
of the Connemara Hotel, C-in-C Road, may be beyond budget
for a long stay, but at least treat yourselves to a dinner in its
Raintree Restaurant, where superb food is graced by authentic
Classical Indian music and dance in a tropical garden. The
world's most magical restaurant!

Nightlife   Classical Indian music and dance in tourist hotels.
Eating out under the stars. Strolling along the beach and
through the bazaars. India is a safer country than many in the
West.

Food   Indian food is by now too familiar to need detailed
description. Just bear in mind that it is usually hotter and spicier
there than the Anglo-Indian food served in Britain. If you have
the choice, ask for dishes without chillis – the tiny green ones
which sear the palate.

Goa is renowned for its seafood: tiger prawns, lobsters and
mackerel, freshly caught and cooked to specification on the
beach. Pork vindaloo and pork sausage (*chourisso*) are specialities
(as Christians, the Goans are the only people in India allowed to
eat pork). The Europeans have taught them to prepare such
delicacies as egg and chips, but the food otherwise is much like
the food elsewhere in India.

The Southern Indian food of Tamil Nadu is based on rice
rather than on the nothern *chapatti*. The most popular dish is the
thali, so called from the metal tray on which it is served – though
in country places, a large banana leaf may replace the tray. Thalis
consist of constantly replenished heaps of rice served with
various types of vegetable curry, pickles, a couple of *puris* or
papadums, a bowl of yoghurt and sometimes a small dessert. The
favourite snacks are *samosas*, now well known in Britain, and
masala dosa, a large thin pancake stuffed with curried vegetables.
Southern *idlis* are tasteless rice dumplings, enlivened with spicy

sauces. Indian sweets really are sweet. Alcohol in Goa is plentiful and cheap. Try *feni*, the local cashew-nut or coconut spirit. Elsewhere in India, beer and spirits are heavily taxed. Indian beers have delightful names such as Kingfisher, Rosy Pelican and Golden Eagle and are expensive in relation to the meals they accompany, though not by Western standards. The term IMFL (Indian Manufactured Foreign Liquor) is used to describe locally produced whisky, brandy and other Western spirits. They are fairly palatable, but beware of headaches! Avoid Indian wines. Goa and Chennai are both on the north–south tea-coffee divide, so both beverages are available. 'Separate tea' or 'tray tea' comes with a pot, a jug of safely boiled milk and a sugar bowl. It is available only in smart hotels. Normally, tea is produced by boiling together water, milk, tea leaves and sugar, then straining the brew into cups. It is a safe drink in a land of unreliably pasteurized milk and, with practice, you may even come to enjoy it!

Tourists and expatriates   India has for years been the favourite destination of the young backpacker, but the major package operators have now begun to bring in groups of older, wealthier tourists from Europe, Australasia and Japan. British people still live, work and finally retire there, as they did before Independence. Of all our former colonies, India is probably the one where the British feel most at home. Our cultures have overlapped and there is a genuine sympathy between our two races.

Leisure activities   The Southern Indians had mighty trading empires long before the arrival of the Europeans. Untouched by the waves of conquerors from the north, the Cholas, Pandyas, Pallavas, Hoysalas and Vijayanagars sculpted their magnificent temples, grew their spices and sandalwood and amassed their wealth. The great temples of Tamil Nadu are easily reached from Chennai, while the magnificent Vijayanagar capital of Hampi is only a train ride from Panaji.

For the sporty, pleasures in Goa are simple – swimming,

fishing and lying under the palms. The beach resorts offer tennis, squash, fitness rooms, waterskiing and parasailing. Chennai is Clubland, with an Anglers' Club, Yacht Club, Boat Club, Gymkhana Club, Riding Club, Cricket Club and Cosmopolitan Club (18-hole golf course). Most clubs admit temporary members. It is the tennis and chess capital of India and the Chepauk Ground caters for India's greatest passion, cricket.

Both Goa and Chennai are so pleasant that it would be easy to put down roots there, but do take advantage of the cheap air and train travel and go exploring, either independently or on the excellent Tourist Office excursions.

FACT FILE

Money The currency is the rupee (Rs), divided into 100 paise. Sterling, dollars, traveller's cheques (American Express and Thomas Cook are the best known) and credit cards present no problems in cities, though banks can take an eternity to process exchanges. As the rupee is fairly stable, it saves time to exchange money in large amounts. All tourists must pay their hotel bills in foreign currency, or have an exchange receipt handy to prove that they have acquired their rupees legitimately. No rupees may be imported or exported. ATMs in cities.

N.B. If you stay in India for more than 180 days, you will need a *tax clearance certificate* to leave the country. This is easily obtained from the Foreign Section of the Income Tax Department in Delhi, Calcutta, Chennai or Mumbai (formerly Bombay) on presentation of your passport, visa and a bundle of bank exchange receipts (to prove that you have been supporting yourself on imported money, not by working illegally). In practice, you will spend a morning acquiring the certificate and will probably not be asked for it on departure, but the process keeps a few tax clerks in work!

Travel documents A full ten-year British passport, valid for at least six months after the intended return date, and a visa (currently £16 for a 6-month tourist visa).

Circulation of traffic   Left-hand side. International road signs.

Electricity supply   Mostly 220v AC, but some areas have DC. Variety of socket sizes and types. Breakdowns and blackouts are frequent, so take a torch.

TV and radio   Some English-language programmes.

Newspapers and books   The *Times of India*, the *Hindu* and the *Indian Express*. The *Illustrated Weekly of India* and *India Today* are the main current affairs magazines. English-language women's and special interest magazines. *Hallo Madras*, a monthly tourist guide. English books are readily available in cities and resorts. In Chennai, the Landmark Bookshop in Apex Plaza and Higginbothams on Mount Road have an excellent selection. The British Council, 737 Mount Road, is worth joining for its library, newspaper reading room and cultural programme.

Time difference   GMT – 6½ hours.

Drinking water   Do not drink tap water. Good hotels and restaurants provide safe boiled or filtered water. Bottled water is plentiful in towns, but you will need Puritabs in the villages.

Inoculations   None required, but seek medical advice. Malaria prophylaxis, TABT (typhoid, parathyphoid and tetanus) and hepatitis A will probably be recommended.

Medical assistance   Doctors and dentists are English-speaking. Christian mission hospitals usually have better facilities than those run by the Government.

Language   Officially Hindi, but English is the *lingua franca*, spoken not only to tourists but as the chief means of communication between, say, speakers of Tamil and Bengali. English is the language of business, education and culture.

Politics   A parliamentary democracy with two Houses, which elect the president and prime minister. The state governments have legislative assemblies.

Religion   India is 80 per cent Hindu, with the largest concentration in the south. Among a bewildering multiplicity of gods, two are of paramount importance in temple worship – Shiva and Vishnu, who has the popular Krishna as one of his manifestations. Some knowledge of the gods and their iconography is essential for serious temple-visiting. Goa is one-third Christian. India is a secular state, which guarantees freedom of worship to all its Hindus, Muslims, Sikhs, Buddhists, Parsees, Jains, Christians and Jews. Shoes must be removed in all temples. The cow is sacred to the Hindu and wanders unmolested through city streets.

Shopping bargains Silks and cottons, which can be tailored cheaply. Carpets, papier mâché, jewellery, leather goods, bronze figures, inlaid marble. The various state emporia, where prices are fixed, are good places to view items from all over the country.

Film Slide film is virtually unobtainable. Print film available and inexpensive.

Miscellaneous Hotel touts besiege the independent traveller on arrival in Panaji and taxi-drivers everywhere earn commission by introducing clients. So have the name and address of your hotel ready and be resolute. Respect Indian modesty. They can just about cope with men in shorts, but women should be well covered off the beach. The Indians pay great attention to the neatness and cleanliness of their own clothes, and dress to kill on formal occasions. The scruffy casual travelling gear of the average Westerner is a source of amazement to them and may result in banishment from smart hotels. Do not become over-anxious about your health. Delhi Belly is notorious, but if you follow the advice in Chapter 8, your problems should be few.

Useful addresses

Government of India Tourist Office, 7 Cork Street, London W1Z 1PB, Tel: 020 7437 3677.

Excellent tourist offices in all Indian cities.

High Commissioner for India, India House, Aldwych, London WC2B 4NA, Tel: 020 7836 8484.

British High Commission, Shantipath, Chanakyapuri, New Delhi, Tel: (11) 687 2161.

British Consulates in Chennai and Mumbai (formerly

Bombay) British Council Libraries in Chennai and Trivandrum.

MADEIRA

Madeira, 'the floating garden', is the peak of a long-extinct volcano surging from the Atlantic seabed off the coast of Morocco. Warmed by the Gulf Stream, with a relatively high humidity, it is amazingly lush in vegetation. Although it is only thirty-six miles long and fourteen miles wide (about the size of the Isle of Wight), it offers every kind of landscape – jagged, cloud-capped mountains, gentler terraced slopes of vines, bananas and sugar-cane, blustery headlands and sheltered bays. Tourism is now the island's main industry and there are modern hotel complexes, restaurants and bars to cater for the most sophisticated tastes, as well as simpler pensions in the old towns. Legend has it that Madeira was discovered in 1346 by two runaway English lovers. The marriage of a number of British troops to Madeiran girls during the Napoleonic Wars strengthened the links between our islands, and the British who winter on Madeira feel very much at home.

A word of warning. The island is one great mountain, with rugged country and steep cobbled streets. Those who like to go exploring will need to be strong walkers with stout hearts and sturdy shoes.

Climate

Maximum and Minimum Coastal Temperatures

Oct	Nov	Dec	Jan	Feb	Mar	Apr
23	22	19	19	18	19	19
18	16	14	13	13	13	14

The warm, sheltered southern coast is divided from the wetter, windier north by a central mountain range with high precipitation.

High season   Winter.

Travelling there   Direct flights from the UK or via Lisbon.

Travelling around   Excellent bus services and inexpensive taxis.

Car hire. The island of Porto Santo with its six miles of sandy beach can be reached by scheduled air service (15 minutes), hydrofoil or boat (3 hours). The crossing may be rough.

Travelling abroad   Nowhere accessible.

Where to stay   Most hotel accommodation is in or near the capital, *Funchal*, which is a convenient base for exploring the island. The Baia de Zarco region around the oldest town, *Machico*, ten miles from Funchal, has the island's largest purpose-built tourist development. There are small, quiet villages, both coastal and inland, for those seeking tranquillity and lower prices.

Accommodation   The island's most famous hotel, Reid's, celebrated its centenary in 1991. Set in semi-tropical gardens on a cliff-top overlooking Funchal Bay, it is beyond the reach of all but the seriously rich for a long-term stay, but tea on the terrace is an affordable pleasure not to be missed. Reid's has now been joined on its cliff-top by a number of modern four- and five-star hotels, with swimming pools, gymnasia, tennis courts, discos, video lounges and a choice of restaurants and bars. Machico has similar hotels and also self-catering aparthotels with all leisure facilities. If you wish to spend the winter in hotels of this standard, you cannot do better than book a long-stay package with a tour operator. Prices begin at about £200 a week per person on half-board terms; self-catering from about £120. Both prices include flights and transfers.

As is clear from their brochures, the major tour operators favour the same few hotels. The Dom Pedro, for example, is used by almost all of them and, apart from the waiters, you would not see a non-English face. But Madeira has many hotels of all categories, a wide choice of pensions and country inns (*estalagems*). Pension prices are in the (€30–50 range for a double room (£20–£33). Winter is high season, so do not expect large reductions on a long stay, though you may be able to negotiate 5 to 10 per cent off, especially a little inland, in villages such as Caniço and San Gonçalo.

As Madeira is such a small island, the independent traveller can explore it all before deciding where to settle for the winter. The obvious and most attractive first base is a hotel in one of the old quarters of Funchal.

Starter hotel

Quinta Penha de França, Rua da Penha de França 2, Funchal. €30. for a double room with breakfast (£20). A quiet oasis with charming gardens near to the centre of Funchal. Seawater swimming pool.

Nightlife   Nightclubs, discos and traditional floor shows in large hotels. Non-residents usually welcome. Nightspots in central Funchal are patronized by the locals as well as by tourists and there is a casino.

Food   Ocean fish and a wide variety of fresh vegetables are the basic ingredients. Try the *espetada* (beef kebabs sizzled over a fire of laurel twigs), *caldeirada* (fish soup), *espada* (black scabbard fish), *bife de atun e milho frito* (tuna fish and fried maize) and *carne vinho e alho* (pickled pork with garlic). Tropical fruits. Most table wines are imported from Portugal, as the famous Madeiras are drunk as aperitifs (*sercial* and *verdelho*) or dessert wines (Bual and Malmsey). There is lager, brandy and aguardente, the local firewater.

Tourists and expatriates   Madeira has long been a favourite winter resort of the British, who throng the island. Few residents, as little suitable property is available for purchase.

Leisure activities   Madeira's volcanic cliffs drop steeply into the sea, so there are no beaches. Swimming-pools and sun-terraces at the hotels and a public lido complex in Funchal. It is splendid walking country and paths through the mountains and woods, following the old irrigation channels (*levadas*), are marked out and graded in difficulty. (See also *Landscapes of Madeira*, Sunflower Books, for detailed itineraries.) There is a 27-hole golf course sixteen miles out of Funchal. Deep-sea fishing, most water sports, riding, tennis. Botanical Gardens in Funchal with orchids, tropical and semi-tropical plants. Rich fifteenth- and seventeenth-century churches and collegiate buildings in Funchal, where the Manueline cathedral is famous for its Moorish ceiling of cedar and ivory. The hair-raising basket toboggan-ride down the cobbled hill from Monte to Funchal. Bridge and bingo in the tourist hotels.

FACT FILE

Money   The currency is the Euro, divided into 100 cents. Sterling and traveller's cheques are easily encashable. Credit and charge cards widely accepted. ATMs in resorts.

Travel documents   A ten-year UK passport gives entitlement to 90 days' stay. Extensions on application to the local police.

Circulation of traffic   Right-hand side. International road signs.

Electricity supply   220v AC. Round two-pin plugs.

Television and radio   Madeira Tourist Radio broadcasts in English.

Newspapers and books   Monthly *Madeira Island Bulletin*.

Time difference   GMT with no seasonal time-changes.

Drinking water   Tap water is safe. Plentiful mineral water.

Inoculations   None required.

Medical assistance   Many English-speaking doctors and dentists. Free emergency out-patient treatment available to British citizens under reciprocal arrangements.

Language   Portuguese. The people do not appreciate being addressed in Spanish, but English is widely spoken.

Politics   Madeira is an autonomous region of the Republic of Portugal and elects its own Assembly.

Religion   Roman Catholic. English mass at Igreja da Penha, Funchal. Anglican church, Rua de Quebra Costas (large English library). Scottish church, Rua do Conselheiro.

Shopping bargains   Embroidery, wickerwork, leather goods, hand-decorated glazed tiles (*azulejos*), Madeira wines.

Film   All types and brands available at roughly UK prices.

Useful addresses

   Portuguese National Tourist Office, 22 Sackville Street, London W1X 1DE, Tel: 020 7494 1441.

Madeira Tourist Information Office, Avenida Arriaga 18, Funchal, Tel: 29057.

Portuguese Consulate General, 62 Brompton Road, London SW3 1BW, Tel: 020 7581 8722.

British Consulate, Rua de Sé 14, Funchal.

MALAYSIA

Malaysia is a federation of thirteen states, eleven of them in the peninsula between Thailand and Singapore and two (Sarawak and Sabah) in East Malaysia, which is the northern part of the island of Borneo. The country has all the natural beauties you would expect of a tropical land: rain forests, hill stations, national parks, palm-fringed beaches of stunning whiteness, seas of translucent blue and even an orang-utan rehabilitation centre. Culturally, it is a vibrant mix of Malay, Chinese, Indian and European. There are museums, temples, mosques and churches in profusion and friendly, cheerful people, for whom English is the chief means of communication! A British Crown Colony until its independence in 1957, Malaysia combines the exotic with the comfortingly familiar. Holiday Inns, Hiltons, porridge and Guinness co-exist happily with traditional Chinese hotels, satay and chrysanthemum tea. Malaysia offers a high standard of living at relatively low prices and must be one of the best choices for a winter escape.

Climate

Coastal Areas

Maximum and Minimum Temperatures

Oct	Nov	Dec	Jan	Feb	Mar	Apr
32	31	32	32	33	33	33
23	23	23	23	23	23	24

Cameron Highlands

Oct	Nov	Dec	Jan	Feb	Mar	Apr
22	22	22	22	22	23	23
14	14	13	13	13	13	14

The west coast wet season is September to December; the east coast and east Malaysia October to February. Showers are usually brief, with sunshine between.

Travelling there   Direct flights from London to Kuala Lumpur and Singapore, with connecting flights to all Malaysian state capitals. Many bargain fares, as Kuala Lumpur and Singapore are on the Australasia routes. Onward flights from Singapore can be expensive and it is often cheaper to cross the straits to Johore Bahru for a Malaysian flight.

Travelling around   Comfortable, modern trains up the west coast from Singapore to Thailand. Excellent bus network. Economical long-distance taxis, which set off from the 'teksi stand' when full. Cycle rickshaws. Car and cycle hire.

Travelling abroad   Thailand and Indonesia are the nearest and simplest to visit, but India, Burma, Hong Kong and the Philippines are also possibilities. Regular boat service from Penang to Chennai; occasional passenger-carrying cargo ships and yachts to neighbouring countries. Visas to these countries can be obtained in advance in London or from the appropriate embassies in Kuala Lumpur. For visits to Singapore, save a fortune by staying in one of Johore Bahru's many good hotels and crossing the Straits bridge daily.

Where to stay   Malaysia has so many hundreds of miles of palm-fringed beach with excellent tourist facilities, that the visitor is spoilt for choice. Though many swear by the relatively undeveloped east coast of the Peninsula, the west coast is the better choice in winter, as it is drier and has much more to offer culturally. *Penang Island*, with its capital Georgetown, is 'the pearl of the Orient'. The first British trading post in the Far East, it has historic buildings and temples, restaurants, shops, markets, botanical gardens, a bird park, a butterfly farm, forest reserves and a Swiss funicular railway up Penang Hill, as well as the obvious beaches, water sports and golf. A 24-hour ferry service operates between the island and mainland Butterworth and there is a new road-bridge. Relaxed, friendly and colourful, Penang is one of the best places in the world to be, with easy communications to other parts of Malaysia.

Kuala Kangsar, a gracious city on a beautiful bend of the Perak River, is a smaller town, in which it would be pleasant to put down roots. There is little action in the town, but Perak State has many attractions.

For those who prefer a cooler climate, the *Cameron Highlands* (4,500–5,500 ft) are easily reached from Kuala Lumpur or Butterworth. They are famous for their riotous vegetation, tea plantations and wild flowers, especially orchids. There are forest and mountain walks, from easy strolls to challenging climbs, waterfalls and an excellent golf course. December and April can be crowded. For the serious great outdoors, try *Sarawak* or *Sabah*. The Malaysia Tourism Promotion Board will advise. Possibilities are white-water rafting, wilderness camping, trekking through the rainforests and cave exploration, but they need to be organized and led by experts.

Accommodation Every category from five-star to quaint, but clean, Chinese-run budget guest houses, where your huge pot of weak China tea is replenished, free of charge, throughout the day. Beaches often have colonies of palm-fringed huts or traditional wooden houses on stilts. The Malaysia Tourism Promotion Board has a special booklet listing approved budget hotels. In smaller towns, always check out the Rest Houses. There were originally built for British officials on tour in the country and are now leased out to Malaysian hoteliers. Usually in the best locations, with views over hills and rivers, they have sitting-rooms, rattan furniture, verandahs and good restaurants. Prices vary, but they can be cheaper than standard hotels and much pleasanter.

Starter hotels On Penang Island there are many beach resorts with splendid facilities. Start in Georgetown, as it is the best base for exploring possibilities, even if you do not wish to stay there long-term.

Oriental Hotel, 105 Penang Road, Georgetown. M$100

nightly for a double room (£16.50) A pleasant, centrally situated hotel at a reasonable price.

At least have tea or a drink at the great Eastern and Oriental ('the old E & O'), one of Somerset Maugham's haunts, even if the cost of a stay is above budget.

Rumah Rehat (the Rest House), Bukit Chandan, Kuala Kangsar, Perak. M$80 for a double room (£13). A remarkably spacious rest house with gardens running down to the Perak River. Good terrace restaurant.

New Garden Inn, Tanah Rata, Cameron Highlands. M$240 a night for a double (£39).

Nightlife   City shops close late and people stroll the streets in the cool of the evening. Night markets, cafés and restaurants. Casinos and discos in the resorts.

Food   Malaysia's food reflects its cultural variety. The indigenous cuisine is rice-based, cooked in coconut oil and served with spicy peanut sauce. *Satay*, small pieces of meat marinated in spices and charcoal-grilled, is the most popular snack. Try *laksa*, a delicious shredded fish soup, with rice noodles, cucumber, pineapple and prawn paste and *rajak*, a salad of flour cake, beansprouts, shredded cucumber, egg, prawn fritters and squid. Tropical fruits and fruit juices. Chinese and Indian settlers run restaurants specializing in their own cuisines. And if you get tired of the exotic, the Malaysians have been well schooled in the art of preparing roast beef and Yorkshire pudding, or porridge and scrambled eggs with a nice pot of tea!

Tourists and expatriates   Most tourists come from Britain and Australasia. Many British work out there for multinational firms or run their own businesses.

Leisure activities   Malaysia had powerful sultanates engaged in Eastern trade long before the arrival of the Europeans in 1509. Portuguese, Dutch and English have all held the ports and left their monuments; there has been Chinese settlement since 1405, when the Ming Admiral Cheng Ho began the conversion of the Malays to Islam; Southern Indians, arriving in the last century to work the rubber plantations, have stayed and made their own contribution. Historically and culturally, Malaysia is a fascinating country to explore. Leisure activities are taken seriously in this prosperous country. The Malayan Nature Society, for instance, organizes trips to view Gould's Frogmouth, the Masked Finfoot, the Scarlet-Rumped Great Slaty and over 250 other exotic species of bird in the national parks and jungles. There are clubs for angling, potholing, scuba diving, photography, 4 × 4 adventure driving, mountaineering, canoeing and, of course, golf. Full details from the special interest brochures of the Malaysia Tourism Promotion Board. Bridge and mahjong.

FACT FILE

Money   The currency is the Malaysian Ringgit (M$), divided into 100 sen. No problems with pounds, dollars, traveller's cheques or credit cards. ATMs in cities.

Travel documents   A full ten-year British passport, valid for 3 months beyond the proposed date of departure. No visa required by UK citizens, and there is currently no limit to the length of time they may stay in Malaysia as tourists.

Circulation of traffic   Left-hand side. International road signs.

Electricity supply   220v AC. A mixture of three-pin flat and two-pin round plugs.

Television and radio   English channels on the local stations.

Newspapers and books   The *New Straits Times* is the old-established English newspaper, but there are many others. English books in all large towns and resorts.

Time difference   GMT + 7 hours.

Drinking water   Tap water is safe in the towns and resorts, but needs to be boiled in the *kampongs* (villages) or up-country.

Inoculations   The Peninsula has a healthy climate, but for East Malaysia malaria prophylaxis is essential. Seek current medical advice before travelling to any part of the country, as the situation can change.

Medical assistance   All doctors, dentists and senior nurses speak

English. The state-run clinics in villages provide good free emergency treatment for visitors. In cities seek private assistance.

Language Officially Bahasa Malay, but English is spoken everywhere. As Malay is written in Roman script, street signs are no problem.

Politics The Federation of Malaysia is a member of the British Commonwealth with a bicameral federal parliament. The Sultans of the thirteen states act as president in rotation. Positive discrimination in favour of the Malay *bumiputra* (sons of the soil) causes some resentment in the other communities, but there is no open hostility.

Religion Islam is the official religion, but the constitution guarantees religious freedom. The Muslim majority respects the minority religions and the festivals of every faith are widely celebrated. There are Christian churches everywhere. Islam is stronger and more orthodox along the east coast and in East Malaysia than in the cosmopolitan West. Decorum in dress is appreciated in this Muslim country and visitors must remove their shoes in mosques, Hindu and Buddhist temples.

Shopping bargains Gold, diamonds and jade from reputable dealers. Pewterware, woodcarving, batik. Prices in stores are fixed; bargaining is customary in markets.

Film Readily available, but more expensive than in the UK. Take a good supply, or hop over to Singapore for bargain photographic equipment of all kinds.

Miscellaneous It is not the custom to tip, even in taxis. In Singapore it is illegal! A 10 per cent service charge may be added in the more expensive hotels and restaurants.

Useful addresses

    Malaysia Tourism Promotion Board, 57 Trafalgar Square, London WC2N 5DU, Tel: 020 7930 7932.

    Tourist offices throughout Malaysia. Excellent literature.

    Malaysian High Commission, 45 Belgrave Square, London SW1X 8QR, Tel: 020 7235 8033.

    British High Commission, 185 Jalan Ampang, 50732 Kuala

Lumpur. Tel: (3) 2170 2200.
British Council Offices and Libraries in Kuala Lumpur and
Penang.

THAILAND

Thailand has rainforests, mountains, pure-white palm-fringed
beaches, turquoise seas and lagoons and a winter climate which
is warm and dry, but not overwhelmingly hot. To these natural
beauties add its courteous, smiling people, who know how to
welcome visitors, temples and palaces, good food, good
communications and hotels of every category, and you have a
wonderful winter destination. The cost of living (outside
Bangkok) is low. Those unused to the East will find Thailand
fascinating in its strangeness, yet reassuring in its comforts and
standards of cleanliness.

In many ways, Thailand has become a victim of its own
success as a tourist mecca. Some resorts are now so crowded that
precious water must be diverted from cultivation to meet the
needs of the hotels and golf courses; near Phuket, the people are
rationed to a few litres a day, so that tourists may enjoy unlimited
baths and showers. And 'sex tourism' has become notorious.
Fortunately, these abuses are limited to the few destinations
favoured by the international tour operators. The rest of
Thailand is free and unspoilt, to be appreciated by the
independent traveller.

Climate
Maximum and Minimum Daily Temperatures
Centre and South

Oct	Nov	Dec	Jan	Feb	Mar	Apr
31	31	31	32	33	34	35
24	22	20	20	22	24	25

Chiang Mai and the North

Oct	Nov	Dec	Jan	Feb	Mar	Apr
31	30	28	29	32	34	36
21	19	15	13	14	17	22

High season   The best season is November to April, after the monsoons, but before the summer heat. August, December and January are the peak months for western tourists.

Travelling there   Direct flights to Bangkok. Many bargain fares, as it is a stop-over on the Australasia routes. Shop around.

Travelling around   Internal flights to resorts. Comfortable trains, especially the old-fashioned sleepers. Good inter-city coaches. Chauffeur-driven cars are almost as cheap as self-drive hire. Three-wheeled motor scooters (*tuk-tuks*) and cycle-rickshaws as well as taxis. Agree the charge first. River-boat services along Bangkok's *khlongs* (canals).

Travelling abroad   Overland to Malaysia and Singapore. Flights out of Bangkok are cheap, making trips to Burma, India and other South-east Asian countries feasible. Visas may be obtained in Bangkok, where necessary.

Where to stay   A week in *Bangkok* at some point is essential, but it is far too crowded and traffic-ridden for a long stay. The seaside and mountain resorts are the places to be. Avoid the once-lovely Pattaya, near to Bangkok, as overpopularity has brought the crowds and the sewage. Royal Hua-Hin, also near the capital, is blighted by day trippers. To find peace and translucent waters, go south down the peninsula towards Malaysia.

The *west coast*: The island (Ko) of *Phuket*, 'the pearl in the Andaman Crown', is the main holiday destination. Its coral reefs offer excellent diving and truly turquoise sea. Chinese and Portuguese influence provide cultural variety and the seafood is superb. Although there is a Club Méditerranée on Kata Beach, Phuket is a large island and there are many other beaches, such as Karon and Surin, which combine tranquillity with good facilities. Mai Khao beach is where the sea-turtles come ashore in the winter to lay their eggs. Ko Phi Phi and other small, idyllic islands can be reached from the port of Krabi. Much of this area, both shores and inland forests, is national parkland. Flights to Phuket from Bangkok.

The *east coast* is more sheltered, with calmer seas, though there is the occasional warm wind in mid-winter. The main resort, *Ko Samui*, with its waterfalls and hidden beaches, still relies more on coconuts than on tourism. Thought by many to be the most beautiful island in South-east Asia, it is the hub of a small archipelago. Most of the other islands are accessible by ferry and some, like Ko Phangan, have beach accommodation convenient for snorkelling on the coral reefs. The economic balance of these islands may soon shift, as Ko Samui now has its airport. If beachcombing palls, there is *Songkla*, further down the coast, where a colourful mix of Thais, Chinese and Malays inhabits a peninsula between a lagoon and the South China Sea. A busy fishing port, Songkla has the intellectual stimulus of a university, research institutes and technical schools; it also has a military academy and a large nursing college. Elegant hotels, historic architecture, a fine white beach and good communications make it an interesting city in its own right and a convenient base for exploration.

Inland: *Chiang Mai* in Northern Thailand is an historic city in the midst of scenic beauty. It is the starting-point for elephant safaris and treks into the hills of the Golden Triangle, the area between Burma and Laos where the opium poppy is still grown by the hill tribes, despite official efforts to suppress the trade. (The poppies bloom in November and December and the air is fresh then for trekking.) Chiang Mai itself has over three hundred temples in its ancient centre, bounded by moats. It is a friendly, cosmopolitan, easy-going city with excellent hotels and restaurants at all price levels. Sukhothai, Thailand's first capital, and the temples of Phitsanuluke are within easy reach.

Accommodation Bangkok and Pattaya apart, Thailand is a country where most of us can afford the multi-starred hotels. Standards are high and building is imaginative. Beach resorts have colonies of well-appointed palm-thatched bungalows, or traditional wooden houses on stilts, as well as excellent four- and five-star hotels. Each of us has a different idea of paradise and it is a good idea to book into a comfortable hotel in Phuket Town or Na Thon, the main town of Ko Samui, and spend a week or two searching for the ideal resort. The price of a thatched hut for two on the beach with a communal outside shower can be as little as £2 a night out of season, while £5 or £6 will pay for private facilities. Hotels come in all price brackets, up to a maximum of about £85 for a luxury double.

Thai travel agents have special discount arrangements with hotels throughout the country and will book you a room in a medium to high category hotel at a better initial rate than you could negotiate yourself. The budget hotels are not usually on their lists and must be approached independently. Haggle over long-stay tariffs, whatever the category of hotel.

Starter hotels   In Bangkok the number and variety of hotels is bewildering. On arrival, go to the wonderfully efficient Hotel Reservation Desk at Don Muang International Airport, where the cheerful girls will suggest a hotel in your price range, book your room and give you the maps and information needed to get there. Do not attempt to wrestle with the complications of this bustling city unaided! For Phuket Town, Na Thon, Songkla and Chiang Mai ask a Bangkok travel agent to make the initial reservation for you. He will be able to book your starter hotel at a discounted rate. Once installed in your chosen resort, begin the search for your long-term accommodation. Consult the local travel agents, who may be able to do a better deal on your behalf, unless you are looking for really cheap accommodation. Na Thon is small enough to go it alone from the start, if you wish. Try the Palace Hotel, 152 Nathon, on the seafront, which has recently been remodelled. From 400 bhts. for a double room (£6).

Nightlife   Notorious in Bangkok and the most fashionable resorts. Elsewhere, there is live music in restaurants, cafés and cocktail bars. Night markets with stalls for dinner as well as bargains. Displays of traditional Thai dancing. Air-conditioned cinemas.

Food   To a base of rice or noodles, the Thais add a variety of fresh vegetables, fish, poultry, pork and beef, cooked in coconut oil and flavoured with lime juice, lemon grass, tamarind, coriander, ginger or a salty fish sauce. Similar in appearance and ingredients to Chinese food, it tends to be hotter and spicier. The tiny green chillis are best pushed to the side of the plate! Tropical fruits and fruit juices. Fish restaurants on the beach, where you choose your fish and the method of cooking. Alcohol is expensive, relative to other prices, as a bottle of Singha beer may cost more than the dinner it accompanies. Local rice whiskey and rum for the bold.

Tourists and expatriates   The tourist trade relies heavily on Australasians, West Coast Americans and Japanese. A few British residents, usually men who have gone out there to work, married a Thai girl and settled down.

Leisure activities   Thailand is the only country in South-east Asia never to have been under foreign domination, so that its culture is uniquely indigenous. The rich variety of temples (*wats*) repays study. Thai boxing (kick boxing) and traditional dancing. Try an authentic Thai massage – the genuine thing is quite different from the services offered in the so-called 'massage parlours'. Water sports of every kind. Hill-walking. Orchids for the botanist. Over fifty excellent golf courses, including a number in Bangkok, Phuket, Songkla and Chiang Mai.

FACT FILE

Money   The currency is the baht (bht), divided into 100 satangs. Thailand is financially sophisticated. No problems in the towns and resorts with currency, traveller's cheques or credit cards. ATMs in cities.

Travel documents   A full British ten-year passport, valid for at least three months after your proposed date of departure from Thailand. A visa is required, which is simply an *entry* visa, normally entitling the visitor to remain for two months in the country. An extension should be requested of the Immigration Officer on arrival in Thailand, who may permit a stay of three months. The Thai Embassy emphasizes that the decision is at the discretion of the Immigration Officer, over whom they have no control. Those wishing to stay for more than two months should apply for a visa entitling them to more than one entry. It will then be a simple matter to cross over into Malaysia (for which full British passport-holders need no visa) and re-enter Thailand for a further two months (or three, if the Immigration Officer authorizes it). To be on the safe side, a triple-entry visa should be obtained, if you are planning to stay for more than four months.

Circulation of traffic Left-hand side. International road signs. Directions in Thai and Roman script.

Electricity supply 220v AC. A mixture of flat three-pin and round two-pin plugs.

Television and radio Frequent English news bulletins on Thai radio.

Newspapers and books The *Bangkok Post*, the *Nation* and *Bangkok World*. Some British books available in Bangkok; popular paperbacks in large resort hotels.

Time difference GMT + 7 hours.

Drinking water Avoid tap water, except in hotels with a purification system. Plentiful mineral water.

Inoculations Up-to-date medical advice essential. Depending on where you propose to go, hepatitis A, cholera, typhoid and malaria prophylaxis may be recommended.

Medical assistance Clean, modern hospitals and clinics. Most doctors and dentists speak English.

Language Thai is a notoriously difficult five-tone language. English is spoken in the service industries and by professional people and students. Those going off the beaten track will need a phrase book which includes written Thai, so that they can point to what they want, if their efforts to pronounce it are not understood. A few simple greetings and courteous phrases are much appreciated.

Politics A constitutional monarchy with an elected bicameral national assembly. The Thais are usually reluctant to discuss politics.

Religion   Buddhist, with Muslim, Hindu, Christian and other minorities. Details of Christian services in Bangkok and elsewhere published in the English-language newspapers. It is the custom for Thai men to become monks for a few months at special periods in their lives, which explains the large numbers of saffron-clad figures.

Shopping bargains   High-quality copies of designer goods, often indistinguishable from the real Gucci or Dior. Thai silks and cottons, tailored to measure. Gems, especially sapphires, rubies and jade – but go to a reputable dealer. Fixed prices in stores; bargaining in the markets.

Film   Available, but more expensive. Take a good supply.

Miscellaneous   Tipping is not customary, except in tourist hotels. One of the charms of Thailand is its very different culture and Westerners must be careful not to give offence unwittingly. Do not speak disparagingly of the monarchy, politicians or religion. Remove shoes in all places of worship and cover head in mosques. Never pose for a photograph before a statue of the Buddha. Never touch anyone's head, even a child's, as the head is sacred; and do not point the lowly feet at anyone. Modesty in dress and behaviour is appreciated. Keep cool; displays of irritation and emotion are counter-productive. These tips and many others are given in useful handouts from the Thai tourist offices.

Useful addresses

Thailand Tourist Office, 49 Albermarle Street, London W1X 3FE, Tel: 020 7499 7679.

Tourist offices throughout Thailand and Tourist Police to help visitors. Comprehensive literature.

The Royal Thai Embassy, 30 Queens Gate, London SW7 5JB. Visa Section Tel: 020 7589 2857.

British Embassy, 1031 Wireless Road, Bangkok 10330. Tel: (2) 305 8333.

British Council, Chulalongkorn Soi 64, Siam Square, Pathumwan, Bangkok 10330.

There are Thai Consulates in Birmingham, Glasgow, Liverpool, Cardiff, Hull and Dublin.

Thai Immigration Office, Soi Suan Phlu, Sathorn Tai Road, Bangkok. (For extension requests and re-entry visas).

USA

The southern USA enjoys superb winter weather, perfect for sitting on the beach, for bathing, windsurfing or playing a round of golf. It also offers fascinating territory to explore – deserts, canyons and vineyards in California and the swamps of the Everglades in Florida. The travel brochures always show frenzied activity, as their main target group is families with young children. Screaming passengers cling to the sides of Disney World rides, bronzed young men paraglide and jetski, and the laser lights pulsate in the discos. But there is another side to it, as is demonstrated by the thousands of Americans who retire there. Away from Orlando and Hollywood, America has the space, freedom and relaxed lifestyle you would expect of a great continent. Visitors from Britain still find car hire, petrol and restaurant meals surprisingly inexpensive. The fact that we share the same language, culture and sets of values makes it a comfortable place to be and the Americans are among the world's friendliest and most outgoing people. An English accent is always a winner! America is home to the British, but on a much larger scale.

Climate

Maximum and Minimum Daily Temperatures

Florida

Oct	Nov	Dec	Jan	Feb	Mar	Apr
28	26	24	23	24	26	27
22	19	17	16	16	18	19

California

Oct	Nov	Dec	Jan	Feb	Mar	Apr
22	21	18	17	17	18	19
14	11	9	8	9	10	12

High season   Christmas. May to October.

Travelling there   Flights to all major cities and resorts. Stand-by, Apex, charters and special offers, so shop around. Liners and cargo ships offer passages to many American ports at fares which range from the astronomical to the surprisingly modest. (See Round-the-World Cruises).

Travelling around   A car is essential, as there is little local transport. Inter-city flights, many discounted. Greyhound and Trailways coaches have good value, unlimited mileage Ameri-passes. Amtrak trains are comfortable, but relatively expensive.

Travelling abroad   Mexico, the Caribbean, the South Pacific. Many short cruises from Florida and California.

Where to stay   For climate, comfort, variety of scenery and interesting occupations, Florida and California are hard to beat. Admittedly, Arizona has the Grand Canyon, the Painted Desert and the Petrified Forest National Park, but it has less to offer generally as a state, and is better visited on excursions.

Florida is a peninsula bounded by the Atlantic on the east and the Gulf of Mexico on the west. Disney World and Cape Canaveral ensure that Orlando, neighbouring Kissimmee and the Atlantic beaches have year-round tourists. The Gulf Coast is more peaceful, though it has flourishing resorts with all amenities. The sands there are softer and whiter, the azure sea almost too brilliant to be true and the coast is less prone to hurricane damage. Inland, the lush wilderness of the Everglades is one of the last refuges for alligators, mountain lions and many species of rare birds. South-west of the mainland lies the Keys, a chain of tiny islands, with golden sands, emerald green mangrove swamps and swarms of tropical fishes around the living coral reefs. All are linked to the mainland by the Overseas

Highway US1. The keys are a birdwatcher's paradise. There are even ospreys nesting on the highway power-poles!

America takes its vacations seriously and all the Florida resorts offer the same high standard of accommodation, the same clean beaches, the same amazing range of leisure activities, which makes it hard to choose between them. On the east coast my own first choice would be *Miami*, an elegant resort with opera, ballet, jazz and the Cuban beat of the refugees from Castro's island. Ocean Drive, with its pastel-painted Art Deco hotels, retains the sophistication of the 1920s and 1930s, when it was the leading Florida resort. As it is the most southerly city it is a good base for visiting the Keys. Cruises leave Miami port for the West Indies, the Bahamas and Mexico. For those who like a true seaside resort, rather than a city with a good beach, *Palm Beach* is a good choice, especially for the golfer, as it has ten golf courses in addition to all the usual water sports. *Cocoa Beach* is another fine resort, quite near to the Kennedy Space Center and within easy reach of Disney World. *Fort Lauderdale* has no fewer than seventy golf courses, but it has become the resort to which students flock in the University vacations, to party on the beach. 'The world's most famous beach', *Daytona*, where Sir Malcolm Campbell made his attempts at the world speed record, is a resort dedicated to the internal combustion engine; it has a Birthplace of Speed Museum and cars are still allowed on the beach. A good place for the fanatical motorist.

On the west coast, *St Petersburg* (known as 'St Pete's') has a 'lively' clientèle. With nearby Busch Gardens, a tropical theme park, and Adventure Island, a waterpark, it offers considerable entertainment for children and young people. Quieter and more exclusive are *Sarasota* and *Sanibel*, one of which would be my own choice.

Of the Florida Keys, the most famous is *Key West*, once the home of Ernest Hemingway and Tennessee Williams. It has pastel-painted clapboard houses, hibiscus, bougainvillea and a high cost of living. Mallory Square at sunset comes alive with trick cyclists, jugglers, magicians and talking dogs. *Key Biscayne* has a world-famous golf course and *Key Largo* makes a speciality of underwater weddings. But *Vaca Key* or *Key Colony* in the centre of the chain would probably be my own choice, as they combine all the best in water sports with proximity to the shops and cinemas of Marathon, the largest town on the Keys. The Keys are really for the divers, snorkellers and sailors. Those with wider interests would be advised to stay on the mainland and make day trips to explore the Keys.

The Florida Everglades are the mangrove swamps and forests bordering a river, in places one hundred miles wide, which flows from Lake Okeechobee in the centre of the state down to the Gulf of Mexico. You can criss-cross the swamps by car along the Tamiami Trail, or explore them silently in a canoe, the best way to see the Florida panthers, alligators, bobcats and black bears. The Port of the Islands resort lies in the heart of the wilderness and it would be a good place to spend a few days, but rather isolated for a whole winter. Only the naturalist would choose the Everglades as a long-stay destination.

California, the Golden State, is the magnet which draws Americans in search of a better life. For the tourist it has everything – a spectacular coastline, orchards and vineyards, the redwoods of the Yosemite and Sequoia National Parks, the mountains of the Sierra Nevada, deserts, sophisticated resorts, music and the arts in Los Angeles, San Francisco and San Diego, the Paul Getty Art Gallery – and Hollywood. Everything is larger than life: Palm Springs alone has eighty golf courses! Yet, though its population doubles in size every twenty years, there are still parts of this vast state where you can motor all day and see scarcely a soul.

San Diego, down near the Mexican border, is California's second city, but it is a garden city with miles of fine beach along its crescent bay and wonderful international cuisine in its Victorian Gaslamp District. It is free of the Los Angeles smog and those seeking a lively city, with culture as well as water sports and golf, would find San Diego an interesting choice. North of Los Angeles, *Santa Monica, Malibu* and *La Jolla* have considerable style, while *Santa Barbara*, though sophisticated, still retains some of the feel and much of the architecture of a Spanish Mission town. All have splendid beaches. Golfers will join ageing Hollywood actors at *Palm Springs*, a green valley lying between the snow-capped San Jacinto Mountains and the desert. The deserts themselves, the national parks and Los Angeles are all more suitable for excursions than for residence.

Accommodation   Prices in the popular resorts are high and since the major travel firms have decided on vigorous promotion of American holidays, mid-range accommodation can sometimes be difficult to find. If you fancy a winter in Palm Springs, Key West, Orlando or similar resorts, it is advisable to book a long-stay package through a travel agent. These packages often include car hire and membership of local golf and country clubs, as well as the flights and transfers. Prices in Palm Springs, for example, start at around £1,350 per person for twenty-eight days, based on two sharing a self-catering, serviced studio apartment, with £229 each for every extra week. These prices include flights and transfers. It would be difficult to beat them for the class of accommodation offered. Most apartment blocks have swimming pools, tennis courts, launderettes, restaurants and shops. There are also special deals for four or six people sharing villas in developments with all amenities. There you would live among American families, as well as fellow tourists. Saga now include Florida and California in their list of long-stay destinations.

Starter hotels   There are so many hotels and motels, literally hundreds in some resorts, that reliable chains are given, rather than individual Starter Hotels. For those who prefer to go it alone, the budget motel chains such as Day's (nineteen of them in Orlando and district alone!), Econolodge, Travelodge and Friendship Inns can cost as little as $30 a night (£20) away from the smarter areas, rising to $65 or thereabouts in fashionable resorts. In the middle price-backet, Howard Johnson, Holiday

Inns, Best Western and Ramada have hotels and motels everywhere, costing around $75 (£50) And you are never far from a top-class Sheraton or Hilton. As the rooms always have two double beds and often an extra divan or two, they are wonderful bargains for families, but rather expensive for the lone traveller. All the budget and middle-range motels advertise their rates on giant hoardings, so that it is easy to cruise along the highway and compare prices.

Prices in California are higher than those in Florida. The same hotel/motel chains are to be found there, but the mid-range Best Westerns in Santa Barbara cost $104–$140 a night (£70–£93) and the cheapest motels in slightly less fashionable Santa Monica cost ($45–60 (£30–£40)

Excellent accommodation at very reasonable prices is often to be found in city centres. Parking difficulties have driven custom to the motels on the outskirts, leaving these once fashionable and famous hotels desperate for trade. Many have become decidedly sleazy, but a few have retained their grace and charm and offer spacious low-cost accommodation, near to all amenities.

Many hotels and motels offer special reduced rates to 'seniors' – and British seniors often qualify. The Third Age lobby is very strong in America. Local tourist offices often have discount vouchers.

Motorhomes   America is superb touring country. For those who enjoy driving, there are now special Motorhome deals: a well-appointed camper (American RV, 'recreational vehicle') with 100 free miles a day, insurance and 24-hour emergency service. The deal may or may not include a cheap flight and the first and last nights in hotels. Motorhomes can be picked up in many cities and the degree of flexibility you can offer as to pick-up point and hire-dates will determine the price. It can be as low as £130 a week, for a 2/3 person RV plus mileage and fuel. Petrol is amazingly cheap by European standards. As this scheme saves on essential car hire and hotel bills, it combines economy with the freedom to go as you please. See America's 'Funway' brochure is a good place to start.

Nightlife　Everything the imagination of man can devise, including bingo, Country and Western, shuffleboard, bridge, bowls, table tennis and darts in the resort hotels. Bingo sessions, open to all, are a speciality of Roman Catholic church halls.

Food　American food consists chiefly of good value steaks, pork chops, fried chicken and hamburgers, but there are also many ethnic restaurants, particularly Italian and Mexican. Portions in all restaurants are very large. Try pancakes and maple syrup for breakfast, often eaten with grilled bacon. Fresh fish by the sea. Good beers and Californian wines. Unlimited coffee is generally on offer in restaurants and a jug of iced water is put on the table as a matter of course.

Tourists and expatriates　Most tourists in America are Americans, especially those from the northern states, known as 'snow bunnies', who flock to the warm south for vacations and retirement. In a recent survey, British children rated America their top choice of holiday destination and it is becoming increasingly popular with British families with young children. A number of all ages are buying property, particularly around Miami and Santa Monica. In fact, Santa Monica has been known for years as 'Little Britain'. Attend a service at St Augustine's by the Sea (Episcopalian) or drop in at 'Ye Olde King's Head' to meet your compatriots.

Leisure activities　Reading the Calendar of Events in your chosen resort is likely to be an exhausting experience in itself! The problem is not what to do, but how to get some respite from your hobbies in areas geared to non-stop recreation. A solitary drive into the desert, or a boat trip through the peace of the Everglades, may be necessary from time to time to restore the balance.

FACT FILE

Money　The currency is the dollar ($), divided into 100 cents. A quarter is 25 cents; a dime is 10 cents; a nickel is 5 cents; and the word 'penny' is sometimes used for a cent. Buy dollar traveller's cheques, as they can be used in shops, hotels and restaurants as normal currency. Changing sterling and sterling traveller's cheques in banks is more difficult than you would imagine. All credit and charge cards acceptable. Few ATMs.

Travel documents   A full ten-year British Citizen passport, valid for at least six months beyond your proposed return date. Under the visa waiver programme, most visitors from Britain no longer need a visa for the first 90 days, but there are exceptions (e.g. British subject passports, Eire passports, those with a criminal record). If your stay will be longer than 90 days, you will need to apply for a visa.

Circulation of traffic   Right-hand side. International road signs. Distances in miles.

Electricity supply   110/120v AC. Round two-pin plugs.

TV and radio   Innumerable channels, all in English.

Newspapers and books   Apart from the *New York Times* and *USA Today*, American papers are strangely lacking in world news. Local, rather than national topics preponderate.

Time difference   Five time-zones. East Coast: GMT – 5 hours. West Coast: GMT – 10 hours.

Drinking water   Tap water and ice are safe. Soft drinks are preferred to mineral water.

Inoculations   None required.

Medical assistance   Excellent, but expensive. Substantial insurance cover essential.

Language   Despite the well-worn joke that we are 'two nations divided by a common language', American English differs in only a few dozen terms, e.g. 'trunk' for car boot, 'yard' for garden, 'faucet' for tap and 'realtor' for estate agent. Half an hour's effort is all that it takes to learn these terms and avoid months of small misunderstandings.

Politics   A federal republic of 50 states with an elected president and two legislative Houses. A member of NATO and one of the five permanent members of the UN Security Council.

Religion   Predominantly Christian. Churches of all denominations, and synagogues.

Shopping bargains   None.

Film   All kinds and brands readily available, at roughly UK prices.

Miscellaneous   America has not gone metric and most Americans have no idea how much a kilo or a litre is. Do not walk at night in downtown Los Angeles.

Useful addresses

American Embassy, 24 Grosvenor Square, London W1A 1AE. Tel: 0906 8200290 for visa enquiries. Tel: 0906 550 8911 for tourist information.

British Embassy, 3100 Massachusetts Ave, NW, Washington DC. 200008. Tel: (202) 588 6500.

British Consulates in Los Angeles, San Francisco, Miami.

ROUND-THE-WORLD CRUISES

Cruises combine the convenience of spending the winter in one place (i.e. in one cabin, with no necessity to pack and unpack) with visiting a wonderful array of exotic locations. Prices range from the astronomical to the surprisingly moderate. If you have dreamed of a 'once in a lifetime' voyage, it may be more affordable than you think.

CRUISE SHIPS

ROUND-THE-WORLD CRUISES

Beginning in Southampton with a send-off by a brass band, you can leave the January snows behind and luxuriate 'around the world in eighty days' on the P.&O. cruise ship, *Aurora*. She travels west from Madeira to the West Indies, sails through the Panama Canal, island-hops across the Pacific to New Zealand and Australia, and sails home via Singapore, India, the Red Sea, the Suez Canal and the Mediterranean. Fares officially begin at £8,315 for a bed in an inside twin with shower and rise to £49,829 per person in a penthouse suite with balcony. The P.&O.'s *Adonia* (the name stands for adults only) offers a 100-night grand voyage to Australia and back, missing out the Americas, but taking in South Africa and many exotic destinations in the Far East. Printed fares begin at £9,729, rising to £48,999 per person in a luxury suite with balcony.

Cunard offer 122 nights on the incomparable *Q.E.2* at fares ranging from £15,499 to £246,249 per person sharing a grand suite. Her itinerary takes in North America, the West Indies, Australasia and a number of the less visited island destinations, such as Sri Lanka, the Seychelles, Mauritius and St Helena. The *Q.E.2* is one of the very few remaining cruise ships where the grade of cabin accommodation determines the restaurant. On most ships these days, there is a free choice.

Round-the-world cruises have become so popular that many competitors have entered the market. The Holland America Line, for example, cruises the world in 108 nights. For British passengers, their *ms Amsterdam* is less convenient, as she sets sail from Fort Lauderdale in Florida and arrives back in San Francisco. But the great attraction is that her voyage takes in Antarctica and the spectacular fjords of Southern Chile – something a bit different from the normal itinerary – by limiting the number of calls in the Far East. Fares range from £23,529 to £126,779. Another imaginative itinerary is offered by the *Saga Rose,* which also sails to the Antarctic, the Falklands and numerous ports in South America, before island-hopping to New Zealand and Australia and returning home via Zanzibar, Cape Town and other African ports. India and the Far East are excluded. A bit less swanky than the Great Ladies of the Sea, the *Saga Rose* is good value for money at £13,699 to £43,999 per person for 107 nights. And she sails from Southampton.

Succulent food, non-stop pampering, entertainments galore and fascinating ports of call make the luxury world cruise truly the trip of a lifetime.

SEGMENTS OF VOYAGES

All the shipping lines market segments of their round-the-world cruises. If you are visiting family in Australia, for instance, you can go one way by sea for the appropriate portion of the full fare, and fly in the other direction. You can sail to Antarctica and fly home from Santiago de Chile. Or you can sail out East and disembark in Penang to spend the rest of the winter in Malaysia. The possibilities are endless.

Obviously, the shipping lines prefer to book in passengers for the full round-the-world voyage, so you need to book segments early.

TRANS-ATLANTIC VOYAGES

Cunard's fabulous new *Queen Mary II* will make her maiden voyage from Southampton to New York in 2004. She will be the largest liner ever built. As she is too wide to pass through the Panama Canal, she will make the Transatlantic run her own, while her sister ship, the *Q.E.II,* will concentrate on round-the-world cruising. Fares have not yet been published, but this would be a spectacular way to start a winter's stay in the United States. There will be special deals for one-way flights, including flights on Concorde.

LOCAL CRUISES

If you are wintering in Florida or California, there are many cruises through the Florida Keys to the West Indies and Mexico, or out to Honolulu and the islands of the South Pacific. These can all be booked locally. Or you could pick up a Cunard, P.&O. or other round-the-world cruise ship in Fort Lauderdale or San Francisco, having made the booking at home.

SPECIAL NOTE ON FARES

Competition out there is fierce. The fares quoted above are no more than starting points, as *no one pays the official printed rates.* Some shipping lines offer reductions of 40 per cent on early bookings. Some offer loyalty discounts or discounts for seniors. Some have cut-price promotions in newspapers, or through societies. Others give vouchers worth £500 for onboard drinks and purchases. So shop around! Your best first step is to contact a specialist cruise agent, who will have inside information on most of the discounts available and be able to guide you through the maze. We are talking big expenditure here, so take no chances. A word with an expert (see below) could save you thousands.

CARGO SHIPS

These provide a different kind of experience. They are not floating hotels, but working ships, where the needs of the few passengers carried are subordinate to the requirements of the freight.

Passengers are very well fed and cared for, but they must be flexible, as delays may occur in the loading of cargo, or itineraries may have to be changed to suit local trading conditions. Life on board a cargo ship is informal, friendly and definitely single class. The facilities, such as the video room, swimming pool and fitness centre, are shared with the officers and crew. Passengers are usually welcome on the bridge, except when the ship is being piloted into port. After a month or so at sea, they come to understand the intricacies of freight handling, the tact required to keep tempers from fraying in a confined space and, in general, get a profound insight into the lives of those whose career is the sea. These voyages are not for people who like non-stop entertainment, but tours are arranged in ports of call and being part of a working ship has its own special interest. As medical services are limited, passengers over a certain age may be asked to produce a health certificate when booking.

SINGLE TRAVELLERS
Cruising on a cargo ship is an excellent choice. Unlike the cruise liners, cargo ships usually have ample single accommodation, which is offered at much the same price as a bed in a double cabin. And the informality of the voyage makes it easy to socialize with other passengers and the members of the crew.

ROUND-THE-WORLD CRUISES
The choice is enormous. The British company, Bank Line, has invested in a new fleet of ships. They offer a voyage of 120 days to New Zealand and back, visiting every island you have ever heard of in the South Pacific and more besides, then returning via Durban or Suez. The fare is £8,500 per person, whether in a double or a single cabin. The German line, Rickmers, also has new ships on its 120-day voyage to Jakarta, Singapore, Hong Kong, Shanghai, Yokohama and New Orleans. Fares are around

£6,000 per person in a double cabin and £7,500 in a single. The C.M.A. C.G.M. French Line, with its French chef, offers New York, Savannah, the South Pacific, New Zealand, Australia, Singapore, Jeddah, Suez and Malta in 84 days for about £5,000 per person in a double cabin and £6,000 in a single. These are just a few examples of the hundreds of possibilities out there. Most of the European cargo ships sail from Tilbury, Hamburg, Antwerp or Le Havre.

SEGMENTS OF VOYAGES
One-way passages and shorter segments can be booked on cargo ships, subject to availability. As cargo ships can accommodate only around six to twelve paying passengers, you should always book early.

LOCAL CRUISES
Short excursions from foreign ports are best researched locally. So if you fancy a trip on a banana boat from Los Angeles, as part of your California winter, explore the possibilities and book your passage out there.

TRAMP STEAMERS
For the totally free and flexible, tramp steamers are wonderful choices. They are 'the taxis of the sea', cruising around looking for business. They ply no fixed routes and sail wherever their cargo takes them. There are not many of them left, but the German Oldendorff Line still operates a large fleet. Itineraries are issued only about a month in advance and can range from Vancouver and Hobart to Easter Island, Mangalore, Macao and Timbuktu. Some of the destinations are so extraordinary that it's quite a challenge to find them on the map!

They are a great way to travel. As the ships are not fully containerized, they have to spend longer in port, unloading and loading their cargo, which gives passengers much more time ashore for sightseeing. Fares start at around £35 a day, all in – and their drinks are the greatest bargains on the high seas, being 'bonded stock', i.e. both duty free and profit free.

THE LANGUAGE OF THE SEA

Fortunately for the British, the language of the sea is English. Whatever the nationality of the ship, whatever flag she sails under, her officers and any of her crew who have contact with passengers, will speak English. This applies to cargo ships and tramp steamers as well as cruise ships. The officers and stewards may be a mixture of German, Polish, Russian and Indian, but they will all be English-speakers. Ships' announcements throughout the world are made in English. And there are no worries about the language of the security guards, as many of them are our own retired Gurkhas.

SHIPPING AGENCIES

There are so many cargo lines, operating so many complicated schedules, that the sensible first step is to consult a specialist shipping agent. It is not feasible to make this kind of booking through your high street travel agent; and trying to go it alone could cost you dear, both in time and money. In fact, it always pays to consult the experts, whether you are dreaming of the top end of the Cunard market or three months tramping the world with Oldendorff.

There are not many of these specialist shipping agencies, but they can be tracked down quite easily in Yellow Pages or on the Internet. They handle bookings on all the passenger cruise lines (with the exception of Saga, who always make their bookings direct). And they keep comprehensive, up-to-date itineraries and fares for the great array of cargo lines, tramp steamers and even scientific research vessels, which carry passengers. They know the ships, they know the discounts on offer and they can advise on the best deals. Your itinerary can be tailor-made to suit your budget and your interests, and the agency can make all the arrangements for you, including connecting flights and insurance.

One of the most helpful and best-informed agencies is The Cruise People Ltd, with offices in London and Toronto. They are at 88 York Street, London W1H 1QT, freephone 0800 526313, **www.cruisepeople.co.uk**. As there are so many possibilities, potential passengers should telephone first for a preliminary chat about the sort of cruise they have in mind, or visit the website, then email them for further details.

ADVENTURE OVERLAND

If you are not too keen on the sea and would rather travel to a wide range of exotic destinations on dry land, a winter escape is a good opportunity to make one of the great overland journeys. There are two major British operators.

Exodus offers an 18-week trip from London to Cape Town for £2,350 (£1,750 from Nairobi); and two tours of South America – 12 weeks for £2,060, or 23 weeks for £3,150. In addition, they have 9 weeks up the Amazon for £1,250. All these prices are exclusive of flights. Travelling overland, often through jungle and wilderness, gives unrivalled insights into the daily lives and culture of people abroad. You live among them instead of flying over the top of them or sailing round them. But Exodus' long overland trips normally involve quite a bit of camping and are only for those who really enjoy, or at least are prepared to tolerate, the rough and tumble of outdoor life, camp cooking and the sharing of chores.

Explore Worldwide is another small-group overland specialist. This company uses hotels, wherever they are available, and caters for a slightly more discriminating market. Their longest trips are shorter than the ones run by Exodus, but they will help you link up itineraries to make a comprehensive tour. You could, for instance, tack one of their cruises up the Nile onto their tour of the temples of Middle Egypt, an expedition to Mt

Sinai, diving off the Red Sea coast and/or a trip out to the desert oases. Between these organized expeditions, you could relax in the perfect winter climate of Luxor, or spend a week by the sea. In South America you could pick and mix from about sixteen different journeys to make your own perfect tour, taking in the Galapagos Islands, the Amazon, a trek along the Inca Trail, a cruise through the fjords of Antarctic Chile or whatever took your fancy. Exodus offers the same facility for linking a group of shorter trips.

SINGLE TRAVELLERS

These overland journeys are good choices, as it is easy to make friends in a small group with similar interests. And there are no expensive single-room supplements. The tour leader arranges for people of the same sex to share.

Exodus Overland Journeys, 9 Weir Road, London SW12 0LT, Tel: 020 8673 0859, **www.exodus.co.uk**.

Explore Worldwide, 1 Frederick Street, Aldershot, Hants, GU11 1LQ, Tel: 01252 760 000, **www.exploreworldwide.com**. Explore produce two brochures, one giving prices inclusive of flights and the other giving the land-only rates.